CIVIL SERVICE

STUDY GUIDE EXAM TEST PREP

Success on Your First Attempt for Clerical, Postal & Police Officer Roles | Tests | Q&A | Extra Content

---

Talon Redwood

EXAM STUDY GUIDE

TABLE OF CONTENTS

INTRODUCTION

Pursuing a career in civil services is more than just a job choice; it's a commitment to public service, a dedication to upholding the values and ideals that form the foundation of the United States. If you're reading this guidebook, chances are you're considering taking the Civil Services Exam or already deep into your preparation. Either way, welcome to a journey that has the potential to shape not just your career but also the future of our great nation.

The Civil Services Exam is a rigorous and comprehensive assessment designed to evaluate an individual's aptitude and readiness for roles within the various arms of the U.S. federal, state, and local governments. The exam's complexity isn't just about testing knowledge but also assessing the analytical abilities, problem-solving skills, and the foundational values expected of civil servants.

Why is preparation so essential for this exam? Apart from the apparent reason for securing a good rank, the preparation process itself instils several qualities in aspirants. It imparts discipline, develops a habit of consistent hard work, and, most importantly, broadens one's horizon about the world and the country's administration. It's about more than memorizing facts or understanding policies. It's about appreciating the larger picture and understanding how individual components contribute to the country's functioning.

This guidebook is designed with the American Civil Services aspirant in mind. Our objective is straightforward: providing clear, concise, and relevant information to aid your preparation. While the guidebook is structured to help you build a solid foundational understanding, we also delve deep into strategies, tips, and nuances distinguishing between a good rank and a great one.

The content in this book is curated and structured to provide a holistic understanding of the subjects at hand. As you navigate through the chapters, you'll find a balanced blend of theoretical knowledge, real-world applications, and critical insights. Every topic is tailored to the U.S. version of the Civil Services Exam, ensuring you get the most relevant and up-to-date information.

But remember, while this guidebook is a powerful tool, it's just that – a tool. Your success in the Civil Services Exam will depend mainly on your dedication, perseverance, and the countless hours you put into mastering the content, practising your skills, and refining your strategies. Approach this guidebook as a companion on your journey, a resource that sheds light on the path ahead, but always remember that the journey is yours. Lastly, a career in the civil services is a privilege and a responsibility.

As you prepare for the exam and look forward to serving your nation, always hold on to the public service ethos. It's not just about clearing an exam but about making a tangible difference in the lives of millions.

Welcome to this transformative journey. Let's embark on it together.

BRIEF DESCRIPTION

The Civil Service System in the U.S. forms the backbone of the federal and state bureaucracies. This system ensures that public servants are selected based on merit and competence rather than political affiliation. One of the most significant mechanisms to ensure this meritocratic selection is the Civil Service Exam. These exams, tailored for various government roles, are critical in recruitment.

Clerical Civil Service Exams

Clerical roles are among the most common positions within the federal and state governments. These positions involve tasks like data entry, file management, and administrative support to higher officials.

- **Exam Structure:** Typically, the clerical civil service exams assess candidates on basic arithmetic, reading comprehension, grammar, and clerical abilities. Candidates may also encounter situational judgment tests that gauge their decision-making skills in administrative contexts.
- **Preparation Tips:** Given the nature of the exam, aspirants should focus on brushing up their numerical skills, enhancing vocabulary, and practicing situational judgment scenarios that align with clerical roles.

Postal Service Exams

The U.S. Postal Service, one of the most iconic institutions in the country, employs hundreds of thousands of workers. To ensure they get the best personnel, they've instituted specific exams.

- **Exam Structure:** The Postal Exam 473 is the primary test for most postal jobs. This exam evaluates skills in addressing, forms completion, coding, memory, and personal characteristics and experiences inventory. The test format includes multiple-choice questions and is timed.
- **Preparation Tips:** Repetition is key. Familiarize yourself with the types of questions on the test. Given the memory test segment, practice exercises that help improve memory retention would be beneficial.

Police Officer Civil Service Exams

Police officers play a critical role in maintaining law and order. Given the responsibility and challenges associated with the job, the recruitment process is rigorous.

- **Exam Structure:** The exact format can vary by state and city, but generally, the police officer civil service exams test for reading comprehension, memory recall, situational judgment, and logical reasoning. Some exams also have a physical fitness component.
- **Preparation Tips**: Beyond academic preparation, aspirants should focus on physical fitness. Engaging in mock situational judgment scenarios to predict and practice optimal responses is also beneficial.

Other Government Roles

Countless other specialized roles within the U.S. government require tailored civil service exams. These roles range from firefighters to sanitation workers, even within specific agencies like the FBI or CIA.

- **Exam Structure:** The format and content vary widely based on the specific role. For instance, a firefighter's exam might test physical strength, stamina, and situational awareness, while an exam for a financial analyst role in a government department could focus on economic understanding and data interpretation.
- **Preparation Tips:** Understand the specific requirements of the role you're targeting. Tailor your preparation accordingly. Maintaining optimal health and fitness is crucial for functions that have physical tests. For more specialized positions, consider seeking out dedicated preparatory materials or courses.

The Importance of Civil Service Exams

The Civil Service Exams serve a two-fold purpose:

- They ensure that the government employs individuals based on merit, capability, and aptitude.
- These exams also prepare the candidates for the roles they're about to undertake, as the very process of preparation imparts crucial skills and knowledge.

Choosing a career in the U.S. civil service is a noble pursuit, but it comes with challenges, primarily in the form of rigorous exams. The key to success lies in understanding the specific requirements of your target role and preparing with dedication and focus. Remember, these exams are not just about securing a job; they're about equipping you with the knowledge and skills to serve your nation effectively.

Whether you're aspiring to be a clerical officer, a mail carrier, a police officer, or any other government professional, approach your preparation with determination. With the right strategy and dedication, you can confidently navigate the Civil Service Exam and embark on a rewarding career in public service.

DISTINCTION BETWEEN FEDERAL AND STATE EXAMS

The United States is built on a federal system of governance, with distinct government layers at the federal (or national) and state levels. As such, when pursuing a career in civil services, one of the primary distinctions you must know is the difference between federal and state civil service exams. Both play crucial roles in the American public sector, yet they are tailored for distinct government sectors and carry unique nuances. This section will delve deep into the differences between these two categories of exams.

The Domain of Operation

Federal Exams: These exams target roles within federal agencies and departments. Federal jobs span the entire country and even overseas for specific departments, like the Department of State. These exams typically aim to recruit personnel for national and international responsibilities, such as the FBI, the Environmental Protection Agency, and the Postal Service.

State Exams: State civil service exams, on the other hand, are administered by individual states and cater to positions within that specific state's government. These could range from state troopers to state health department officials, and these jobs primarily serve the residents of that particular state.

The Scope and Nature of Responsibilities

Federal Exams: Jobs at the federal level often deal with broader national issues and policies. For instance, a job with the Federal Communications Commission might involve setting nationwide broadcasting standards.

State Exams: State roles, conversely, deal with issues that are more localized and pertinent to that state's demographics, economy, and culture. A job in California's state government might focus on wildfire prevention, while one in Florida might revolve around hurricane preparedness.

Exam Structure and Content

Federal Exams: Due to the broad and national scope of federal roles, these exams are more generalized and are designed to assess foundational skills universally applicable across the country. They often include sections on federal laws, policies, and current national events.

State Exams: State exams can be more specialized, reflecting that state's unique needs and challenges. They often include questions about the state's history, specific laws, and governmental structure.

Eligibility Criteria

Federal Exams: Generally, eligibility for federal jobs requires U.S. citizenship, but there are exceptions. The federal government also often has more stringent security clearance requirements, especially for roles related to national security.

State Exams: While most state jobs also require U.S. citizenship, some positions, especially at the entry level, might be open to non-citizen permanent residents. Each state has its criteria and might also have residency requirements.

Application and Recruitment Process

Federal Exams: Federal job openings are typically posted on the USAJobs website, the federal government's official employment site. Applicants can search for jobs, post resumes, and apply directly through this portal.

State Exams: Each state will have its own job portal or system for posting job vacancies. For example, the State of New York uses the New York State Department of Civil Service website to post vacancies and exam announcements.

Advancement and Transfers

Federal Exams: Given the national scope of federal jobs, there's often more opportunity for transfers between states or even internationally without switching employers.

State Exams: Advancements within state jobs are generally localized to that state. If one wants to transfer to a similar role in another state, they would likely have to undergo a new application and another exam in the new form.

Compensation and Benefits

Federal Exams: Federal employees often enjoy comprehensive benefits, including health insurance, retirement plans, and more. Federal salaries and benefits are standardized across agencies but can vary based on location, especially if living costs are higher.

State Exams: Compensation for state jobs varies widely from one state to another. Benefits are generally competitive but might not be as uniform as federal benefits. Each state determines its salary scales and benefits packages.

The distinction between federal and state exams reflects the United States' layered system of governance. While both tiers of government are critical, they serve different roles and have unique challenges and priorities. As an aspirant, understanding these differences is crucial. It guides your preparation strategy and helps you align your career aspirations with the right tier of government, ensuring a fulfilling and impactful career in the American civil service.

In summary, while federal and state exams lead to rewarding careers in public service, they cater to different spheres of governance. As a potential civil servant, your choice should be informed by your career goals, the scale of impact you want to have, and where you want to reside and work.

EXAM STRUCTURE

When embarking on the journey to become a civil servant, one of the most critical aspects to familiarize oneself with is the exam structure. Knowing the exam layout not only aids in targeted preparation but also boosts confidence on the test day.

Sections & Segments

Civil Service Exams typically comprise multiple sections, each targeting a distinct skill set. Common sections include:

1. **Reading Comprehension:** This assesses the ability to understand and interpret written information, often pertinent to governmental roles.
2. **Numerical Ability:** Here, basic arithmetic, statistics, or even budgeting scenarios might be tested.
3. **Situational Judgment:** Real-world scenarios where decision-making skills, ethics, and job-specific knowledge are evaluated.
4. **Logical Reasoning:** Candidates' ability to think critically, discern patterns, and make logical conclusions is tested.

Question Format

Different types of questions can appear, such as multiple-choice, true/false, short answers, or essay-type questions. Multiple-choice is prevalent due to its objective nature, but essay-type questions might be present in higher-level exams to gauge the depth of understanding or written communication skills.

Time Duration: The exam duration varies, but most are designed to assess knowledge and time management skills. Depending on the complexity, candidates might get between 1 to 3 minutes per question.

Scoring Mechanism: Knowing if there's a negative marking for incorrect answers is essential. Some exams subtract points for wrong answers to discourage guessing, while others might not. Knowing this can shape your strategy on whether to attempt uncertain questions.

Practical Components: For specific roles, like police officers or firefighters, there might be physical tests or practical demonstrations of skill. These components evaluate real-world capabilities and readiness for the job.

Understanding the exam structure is akin to knowing the battleground before a strategic game. Familiarizing yourself with sections, question formats, time constraints, and scoring mechanisms will set you up for a more focused preparation and a confident execution on the exam day. As the adage goes, "forewarned is forearmed," and this couldn't be more accurate in the world of civil service exams.

OVERVIEW OF TYPICAL FORMATS

Civil Service Exams, designed to gauge the breadth and depth of a candidate's knowledge and abilities, incorporate various question formats to ensure a holistic assessment. Each form serves a unique purpose, challenging different skills or proficiencies. Here's an in-depth look at some of the most common conditions.

Multiple Choice Questions (MCQs)

- **Overview:** This is the most prevalent format due to its straightforward nature and easy scoring. A typical MCQ presents a question or statement and several options, usually four or five, of which only one is correct.

- **Purpose:** MCQs test foundational knowledge and recall. They can range from simple factual questions to more complex ones requiring analysis or interpretation.

- **Strategy:** Read all options before selecting an answer. Sometimes, options can be similar, or "all of the above" choices may exist. Look for keywords and be wary of absolutes like "always" or "never."

- **Advantages:** It provides quick and objective scoring.

- **Drawbacks:** There's a risk of guessing, and it needs to gauge the depth of understanding or written expression.

Essay Questions

- **Overview:** Candidates are required to provide a detailed written response to a prompt. This might involve discussing a topic, arguing a position, or analyzing a scenario.

- **Purpose:** Essays measure depth of understanding, critical thinking, and written communication skills. They can also assess candidates' ability to organize their thoughts coherently and present a well-structured argument.

- **Strategy:** Plan before you start writing. Outline your main points, and ensure your essay has a clear introduction, body, and conclusion. Be concise clear, and avoid unnecessary jargon.

- **Advantages:** Showcases analytical and writing skills; allows for personalized expression.

- **Drawbacks:** Subjective scoring can lead to variability in grading, and it's time-consuming to write and grade.

Scenario-Based Questions

- **Overview:** These questions present hypothetical but realistic situations that a candidate might encounter in their job role. The candidate's task is to choose the best response from the given options or describe how they would handle the situation.

- **Purpose:** Evaluate situational judgment, decision-making abilities, interpersonal skills, and role-related expertise. It can also test ethics and values in certain situations.

- **Strategy:** Put yourself in the described scenario and think practically. Consider your choice's immediate and long-term effects, and always lean toward ethical and sustainable solutions.

- **Advantages:** Tests real-world application of knowledge and skills; simulates on-the-job decision-making.

- **Drawbacks:** Responses can be subjective, and there may be multiple " right " approaches.

Tips for Tackling Different Question Formats

- **Time Management:** Allocate time wisely. While MCQs might take less time, essays and scenario-based questions require thought and elaboration. Keep track of the time and ensure you answer all sections.

- **Understand the Question:** Before attempting an answer, ensure you've thoroughly understood what's being asked. Reading or understanding a question can lead to lost marks.

- **Practice Regularly:** Familiarity breeds confidence. Regular practice sessions, especially with time constraints, can simulate the actual exam environment and help reduce anxiety.

- **Review:** If time permits, review your answers, especially essay-type responses. Correct any glaring errors, and ensure your writing is legible.

A robust grasp of the different question formats and strategies to tackle them is essential for success in Civil Service Exams. Whether it's the brevity of MCQs, the depth of essays, or the realism of scenario-based questions, each type offers a unique lens into a candidate's capabilities. Remember, the exam doesn't just test what you know but how you apply what you know. Equip yourself with knowledge and strategy, and you'll be well-positioned to excel.

STUDY MATERIAL AND PREPARATION

Arming oneself with suitable study materials and adhering to a structured preparation strategy is crucial to excel in the Civil Service Exams. The broad nature of these exams requires systematic planning and a blend of different resources to ensure a comprehensive grasp of the content. Here's a brief guide to get you on track.

Textbooks and Guides: Begin with textbooks and guides specifically designed for the Civil Service Exams. These offer subject matter content and often include practice questions, sample tests, and explanations. Some renowned publishers and authors have dedicated series for various roles within the civil service, so choosing one tailored to your specific examination can be beneficial.

Online Resources: The digital age has blessed us with many online study platforms, forums, and courses. Websites dedicated to civil service preparation often offer updated content, interactive quizzes, and mock tests. Join discussions or online study groups to discuss doubts, share resources, and gain perspectives from fellow aspirants.

Workshops and Classes: Consider enrolling in preparatory classes or workshops. These provide structured learning, expert guidance, and regular assessments. Interacting with instructors can clarify complex topics, while peer discussions can stimulate motivation and new insights.

Practice Tests: Simulating the exam environment is crucial. Regularly take practice tests to gauge your preparation level, manage time better, and identify areas that need more attention.

Daily Schedule: Allocate specific hours daily for study, ensuring a balance between different subjects. Incorporate short breaks to prevent burnout. A consistent routine helps in retaining information and maintaining focus.

Successful preparation for the Civil Service Exams isn't merely about the hours put in but the quality and strategy of those hours. By leveraging a combination of textbooks, online resources, classes, and regular practice, aspirants can build a solid foundation. Remember, while self-study is the bedrock, seeking guidance, staying updated, and common practice will set you apart.

GENERAL KNOWLEDGE

In the vast landscape of the Civil Service Exams, a segment stands prominent and indispensable: General Knowledge (GK). It's more than just a test of memory; it gauges an aspirant's awareness of the world around them, reflecting their readiness to serve in roles that demand informed decision-making. Within the pages of this guidebook, "General Knowledge" isn't just a chapter—it's an invitation to understand the intricacies of society, politics, history, and more.

As we delve deeper into this realm, readers will discover the key areas to focus on and the interconnectedness of global events and local implications, sculpting an informed and proactive civil servant for tomorrow.

Critical Events in the U.S. History

1. **The American Revolution (1775-1783):** Sparked by growing discontent with British rule, the 13 American colonies embarked on a revolution. Battles such as Lexington and Concord and the surrender at Yorktown culminated in America's independence.

2. **The Civil War (1861-1865):** A defining moment, this war was primarily over the institution of slavery. Pitting the North against the South, the conflict ended with the Confederacy's surrender, marking the abolishment of slavery.

3. **World Wars:** The U.S. played pivotal roles in both World Wars, entering World War I in 1917 and World War II after the Pearl Harbor attack in 1941. Both wars saw America emerging as a global power.

4. **Civil Rights Movement (1950s-1960s):** A struggle for racial equality, marked by significant events like the Montgomery Bus Boycott, the March on Washington, and Martin Luther King Jr.'s "I Have a Dream" speech.

5. **Moon Landing (1969):** The Apollo 11 mission successfully landed the first humans on the Moon, exemplifying American innovation.

Founding Documents

1. **The Declaration of Independence (1776):** Authored primarily by Thomas Jefferson, it declared the 13 colonies' independence from Britain. It proclaimed the inherent rights of individuals, emphasizing life, liberty, and the pursuit of happiness.

2. **The U.S. Constitution (1787):** The nation's fundamental law established America's government structure. With its seven articles and subsequent amendments, it guarantees liberties and rights.

3. **The Bill of Rights (1791):** The first ten amendments to the Constitution ensured personal freedoms, clear limitations on government power, and rights not explicitly mentioned in the Constitution.

Significant Figures

1. **George Washington:** The first U.S. President and a key figure in the American Revolution, Washington set numerous presidential precedents.

2. **Abraham Lincoln:** Serving during the tumultuous Civil War, Lincoln's leadership preserved the Union and led to the abolition of slavery.

3. **Martin Luther King Jr.:** A beacon in the Civil Rights Movement, King championed non-violent protests and delivered powerful speeches advocating racial equality.

4. **Susan B. Anthony:** A pivotal figure in the women's suffrage movement, Anthony played a significant role in granting women the right to vote.

5. **Franklin D. Roosevelt:** The only president to serve four terms, Roosevelt led the country through the Great Depression and World War II with his New Deal programs.

Here are appropriate details of some points mentioned above.

Critical Events in the U.S. History

The American Revolution (1775-1783)

The American Revolution emerged from growing tensions between the 13 American colonies and the British Crown. Rooted in economic strife and cries of "no taxation without representation," the colonies began to push back against British authority. The first shots were fired in Lexington and Concord, setting off a chain of battles and skirmishes that spanned eight years. Events such as the winter at Valley Forge tested the mettle of the American soldiers, while the decisive victory at Saratoga showcased the possibility of a colonial win. The war's culmination at Yorktown, marked by the British army's surrender, paved the way for the Treaty of Paris in 1783. This treaty formally recognized the United States as independent from British rule.

The Civil War (1861-1865)

Often described as America's bloodiest conflict, the Civil War erupted primarily over deep-rooted disputes about slavery and states' rights. The industrial North, aiming for a unionized nation and abolition, stood in stark contrast to the agrarian South, which depended heavily on slavery for its economy. Noteworthy confrontations like the Battle of Gettysburg saw significant losses on both sides, but ultimately, the North's resources and workforce dominated. President Abraham Lincoln's Emancipation Proclamation declared the freedom of all enslaved people in Confederate-held territory. The war ended with the South's surrender at Appomattox Court House in 1865. The aftermath, termed the Reconstruction Era, was a tumultuous period of rebuilding the South and integrating African Americans into a free society.

World Wars

In World War I, the assassination of Archduke Franz Ferdinand set off a series of alliances, drawing multiple countries into the conflict. Though initially neutral, America entered the fray in 1917, swayed by attacks on its ships and the Zimmermann Telegram. Their involvement bolstered the Allies, leading to an eventual victory. The Treaty of Versailles formally ended the war, placing heavy reparations on Germany.

By World War II, global tensions reignited. The U.S. maintained neutrality until the 1941 attack on Pearl Harbor by Japan. Joining the Allies, the U.S. combated Axis powers across multiple fronts. From storming the beaches of Normandy on D-Day to the Pacific Island hopping campaigns, America played a pivotal role. The conflict concluded in 1945 with the unconditional surrender of Nazi Germany and, after the dropping of atomic bombs, Imperial Japan.

Civil Rights Movement (1950s-1960s)

A century post-Civil War, racial segregation and discrimination against African Americans remained prevalent. The Civil Rights Movement, a non-violent protest led by figures like Martin Luther King Jr., sought to overturn these racial injustices. Landmark events, from the Montgomery Bus Boycott instigated by Rosa Parks' defiance to King's iconic "I Have a Dream" speech during the 1963 March on Washington, shaped the era. The culmination was the Civil Rights Act of 1964, which outlawed discrimination based on race, color, religion, sex, or national origin.

Founding Documents

The Declaration of Independence (1776)

This revolutionary document, drafted primarily by Thomas Jefferson, proclaimed the American colonies' break from British rule. Expressing grievances against King George III, the Declaration emphasized unalienable rights, such as life, liberty, and the pursuit of happiness. Beyond its immediate political ramifications, the Declaration is a philosophical bedrock for the nation's values.

The U.S. Constitution (1787)

Post-Revolution, America's first governing document, the Articles of Confederation, proved weak. The Constitution, crafted in 1787, outlined a more robust federal system. It introduced a tripartite government structure — Executive, Legislative, and Judicial — with a system of checks and balances. It remains the definitive guide for U.S. governance.

The Bill of Rights (1791)

The first ten amendments to the Constitution, collectively termed the Bill of Rights, were introduced to address concerns about individual liberties. These amendments safeguard freedoms ranging from speech and assembly to protections against unwarranted searches or seizures.

Significant Figures

George Washington: Regarded as the "Father of His Country," George Washington's leadership during the American Revolution was instrumental. Later, as the inaugural U.S. President, Washington's policies and actions set foundational precedents for the office. His voluntary decision to step down after two terms epitomized his commitment to a democratic republic.

Abraham Lincoln: Serving amidst the turmoil of the Civil War, President Lincoln is revered for his leadership in preserving the Union. His Emancipation Proclamation and subsequent push for the 13th Amendment marked the end of slavery in America. Though his life was tragically cut short by assassination, Lincoln's legacy in American civil rights is unparalleled.

Martin Luther King Jr.: Championing civil rights through non-violent means, Dr. King's influence during the 1960s was profound. His eloquence, showcased in speeches like "I Have a Dream," alongside his commitment to peaceful protests, advanced the cause of racial equality in America.

U.S. GOVERNMENT: STRUCTURE, BRANCHES, STATE VS. FEDERAL ROLES

The United States of America boasts a federal system of government, a unique blend of centralized national authority and individual state rights. Rooted in the U.S. Constitution, this system establishes a balance of power, ensuring that no single entity overpowers another. The Founding Fathers, inspired by European Enlightenment ideas and wary of Britain's monarchical rule, conceptualized a government where powers were explicitly separated and systematically checked.

The Three Branches of Government

- **Executive Branch:** The executive branch is the administrative arm of the federal government, headed by the president of the United States. The president's duties encompass being the Commander-in-Chief of the armed forces, signing or vetoing legislation, appointing federal officials, and conducting diplomatic relations with other countries. Assisting the president in these duties is the Vice President and the President's Cabinet, which consists of the heads of 15 executive departments, such as the Department of State, the Department of Defense, and the Department of Treasury. The Executive Branch also encompasses numerous agencies, bureaus, and commissions that administer laws, provide services, and enforce federal regulations.
- **Legislative Branch:** The United States Congress, consisting of the Senate and the House of Representatives, forms the Legislative Branch. Its primary duty is to make laws. Each state, irrespective of its population, is represented by two senators in the Senate. In contrast, the House of Representatives assigns seats based on population, with larger states having more representatives.
- The process of law-making is intricate. Once introduced in either house, a bill must pass through various committees, be debated, amended, and approved by both houses. Once the Senate and House approve the bill, it's sent to the president. The president can either sign it into law or veto it. However, Congress can override a presidential veto with a two-thirds majority vote from both houses.
- **Judicial Branch:** The Judicial Branch interprets the laws, ensuring they adhere to the Constitution. At its apex is the Supreme Court, consisting of nine justices: one Chief Justice and eight Associate Justices. The president nominates these justices, but their appointment requires Senate confirmation.

The federal court system also includes Circuit Courts of Appeals and District Courts. While the Supreme Court reviews select cases, the lower federal courts handle various disputes, from civil lawsuits to criminal prosecutions.

The Checks and Balances System:

This intricate system ensures that each branch of government can monitor and limit the other branches' functions, preventing any extension from gaining absolute power. For instance:

1. The executive can veto Congressional legislation.

2. The Legislature can impeach the president and override vetoes.

3. The Judiciary can declare laws or executive actions unconstitutional.

4. The president nominates Supreme Court Justices, but the Senate must approve them.

State vs. Federal Roles: The U.S. Constitution delineates the powers accorded to the federal government; any powers not explicitly granted to the national government are reserved for the states.

Federal Roles: Federal authority encompasses areas that require a united front, such as defense, foreign policy, and interstate commerce. Federal agencies, like the FBI or the EPA, work within this scope, enforcing national laws and regulations.

State Roles: States possess a significant amount of autonomy. They can create laws, have their executive, legislative, and judicial structures, and even have their constitutions, as long as they don't contradict the U.S. Constitution. Issues like education, local law enforcement, and infrastructure broadly fall under state jurisdiction.

Concurrent Powers: Some responsibilities are shared. Both state and federal governments can levy taxes, build roads, or establish courts. This often results in a layered system where state and national entities operate simultaneously.

Conflicts Between State and Federal Law: When state and federal laws clash, the Constitution's Supremacy Clause dictates that federal law takes precedence. This principle was affirmed in landmark cases like McCulloch v. Maryland (1819) and continues to be a point of contention in modern politics.

Understanding the structure and intricacies of the U.S. government is essential for aspiring civil servants and every American citizen. This system, with its deliberate checks and balances, was crafted to disperse power, safeguard liberties, and ensure the nation's enduring stability. Whether it's the president issuing an executive order, a state legislature crafting an education policy, or the Supreme Court deciding on a constitutional matter, every action is a testament to the Founding Fathers' vision and the living document that is the U.S. Constitution.

CURRENT EVENTS: IMPORTANT NATIONAL EVENTS AND ISSUES

The United States, given its global standing, witnesses a constant whirlwind of events that have both national and international implications. While capturing every significant occurrence in a singular section is impossible, understanding the broader themes and key events of recent times offers invaluable insights. In the context of civil service exams, possessing a clear grasp of contemporary issues is imperative.

The Digital Age and Big Tech

The 21st century saw an unprecedented rise in the influence of technology giants such as Google, Facebook (now Meta), Apple, Amazon, and Microsoft. Their growth brought forth concerns:

- **Data Privacy:** The Cambridge Analytica scandal unveiled vulnerabilities around personal data and its potential misuse in shaping democratic processes.
- **Antitrust Issues:** The monopolistic behaviors of these companies have become focal points of debate, leading to Congressional hearings and discussions on the possible break-up of these tech conglomerates.
- **Social Media & Democracy:** The role of platforms like Twitter and Facebook in spreading misinformation, influencing elections, and potentially inciting violence, such as the January 6, 2021, U.S. Capitol attack, has become a significant concern.

Climate Change and Environmental Concerns

As global temperatures rise, America grapples with:

- **Natural Disasters:** From hurricanes in the Gulf Coast to wildfires in the West, the increasing intensity of these events underscores the urgency of climate action.
- **Paris Agreement:** After briefly exiting the Paris Climate Accord, the U.S. rejoined, signaling a renewed commitment to global environmental endeavors.
- **Green New Deal:** This proposed package aims to address climate change and economic inequalities but has sparked intense debates regarding its feasibility and implications.

Healthcare

- **COVID-19 Pandemic:** The outbreak began in late 2019 and threw the world into disarray. America's handling of the crisis, from initial responses, development, and distribution of vaccines to economic relief packages, has been a significant point of discussion.
- **Affordable Care Act (ACA):** Often dubbed "Obamacare," the ACA has remained contentious. Attempts to repeal, replace, or modify it continue to divide lawmakers.

Social Justice Movements

- **Black Lives Matter (BLM):** Sparked by police-related incidents, including the deaths of George Floyd and Breonna Taylor, BLM became a global movement advocating for the rights of Black individuals.
- **Asian and Pacific Islander Hate Crimes:** A surge in violence against the Asian community, exacerbated during the pandemic, led to nationwide calls for awareness and legislative action.

Economic Considerations

- **Trade Wars:** The U.S., under President Donald Trump, engaged in significant tariff exchanges with nations, particularly China, shaking global economic frameworks.
- **Inflation and Economic Recovery:** Post-pandemic economic revitalization, coupled with supply chain issues, resulted in noticeable inflation, impacting households and policies.

Immigration and Border Security: America's southern border and immigration policies, including DACA (Deferred Action for Childhood Arrivals) and detention practices, have remained under scrutiny.

Gun Control and Second Amendment Rights: Mass shootings, from school premises to public events, perpetually reignite debates around gun regulations and interpreting the Second Amendment.

Foreign Relations

- **Afghanistan:** The U.S.'s withdrawal in 2021, ending a 20-year military involvement, and the subsequent takeover by the Taliban became global focal points.
- **U.S.-China Relations:** From economic competition and technological advancements (like 5G) to human rights issues in places like Hong Kong and Xinjiang, the dynamics between these superpowers profoundly influence global geopolitics.

Infrastructure and Development

The bipartisan Infrastructure Investment and Jobs Act focuses on revitalizing America's aging infrastructure, from roads and bridges to expanding broadband access.

Staying updated with current events is more than about passing exams; it's about being an informed citizen in a constantly evolving nation. The above encapsulates only a fraction of ongoing events and issues. Yet, they offer a roadmap to America's multifaceted challenges and opportunities. Aspiring civil servants must dive deeper, critically assess sources, and always be ready to adapt their understanding in this dynamic environment.

OFFICE SKILLS

In civil services, understanding governmental structures and national events is undoubtedly essential. However, a robust set of office skills is equally critical to the efficacy of any civil servant. These foundational capabilities ensure daily operations run smoothly and individuals can collaborate, manage, and execute tasks professionally. As the future backbone of our government's administrative functions, mastering these skills is paramount for every aspirant.

Communication Skills

Central to any office setting is the art of communication. Civil servants often liaise between departments, present information to superiors, or address the public. Clear and concise verbal and written communication skills are pivotal. This includes crafting professional emails, drafting reports, giving presentations, and participating in meetings. Active listening, too, is vital, ensuring that one understands directives and feedback accurately.

Time Management: The vast and varied responsibilities within the civil services demand impeccable time management. Balancing tasks, setting priorities, and adhering to deadlines is fundamental. Tools like calendars, digital task trackers, or even traditional to-do lists can be invaluable. Additionally, understanding when and how to delegate can also optimize productivity.

Digital Proficiency: Working knowledge of commonly used software and platforms is non-negotiable in today's digital age. This ranges from word processors like Microsoft Word to spreadsheet tools like Excel. As governmental systems increasingly migrate to digital platforms, being adept at navigating databases, utilizing cloud storage, and understanding basic digital security protocols becomes essential.

Organizational Skills: An organized workspace is emblematic of a methodical mind. The ability to systematically categorize information, manage files, or maintain a tidy desk can significantly enhance efficiency. This could translate to faster retrieval of vital documents or more streamlined intra-departmental processes for civil servants.

Problem-solving and Critical Thinking: While routine is a significant aspect of office life, unforeseen challenges are inevitable. A civil servant's ability to think on their feet, assess situations critically, and find viable solutions is indispensable. This could involve mediating conflicts, navigating bureaucratic hurdles, or addressing public grievances.

Teamwork and Collaboration: The government operates as an intricate web of interconnected departments and teams. Being a team player, understanding group dynamics, understanding when to lead and when to follow, and valuing diverse perspectives are skills that foster harmony and productivity in such a complex environment.

Adaptability

The governmental landscape is ever-evolving, influenced by political shifts, policy changes, and global events. A successful civil servant can quickly adapt to these changes, embrace new directives, and continually update their skill set to remain relevant.

Office skills, while seemingly basic, are the undercurrents that drive the machinery of our government. They ensure that policies are formulated and effectively implemented, that departments don't function in silos but as cohesive units, and that the vast apparatus of the civil services remains approachable and efficient for the public. For those looking to ace their civil services exams and excel in their subsequent roles, investing time in honing these skills is as crucial as understanding the intricacies of our Constitution or the currents of contemporary events.

Computer Literacy: Basic Software Tools, Email, and Internet Usage

In an era marked by rapid technological advancements, computer literacy has transitioned from a valuable skill to an essential one, especially within civil services. It's not just about being able to turn on a computer; it's about using technology as a tool to work more effectively and efficiently. Let's delve deep into the world of computer literacy, emphasizing essential software tools, email, and internet usage.

Understanding Computer Literacy

Computer literacy goes beyond the mere ability to use a computer. It encapsulates the understanding and practical application of various software tools, the internet, and electronic communication forms like email.

The Operating System

Understanding your computer's operating system (OS) is foundational whether you're using Windows, macOS, or Linux. It's the software that runs your computer.

- **Basics of Navigation:** Learning how to navigate folders, manage files, install and uninstall applications, and adjust settings is crucial.
- 3. Basic Software Tools
- **Word Processors (e.g., Microsoft Word, Google Docs):** These are used for drafting documents, reports, and letters. Features to master include formatting text, creating tables, and incorporating graphics.

- **Spreadsheets (e.g., Microsoft Excel, Google Sheets):** Data management, budgeting, and analytics are essential. Understanding functions creating charts and pivot tables can significantly enhance data interpretation.

- **Presentation Software (e.g., Microsoft PowerPoint, Google Slides):** Used for visual displays, especially during meetings or training sessions. Incorporating multimedia, using transitions, and mastering design elements can help create compelling presentations.

- **Database Management (e.g., Microsoft Access):** Storing, organizing, and retrieving data becomes efficient with these tools. Understanding basic queries and structuring data is essential.

Email – The Keystone of Professional Communication

- **Setting Up & Managing Accounts:** Whether you use Outlook, Gmail, or another service, understanding how to set up an account, organize your inbox, and manage settings is foundational.

- **Crafting Professional Emails:** This involves more than just typing a message. It's about understanding professional correspondence's tone, structure, and etiquette.

- **Attachments & Downloads:** Knowing how to attach files to emails, download, and organize received extensions securely is a daily requirement.

- **Safety and Security:** Recognizing signs of phishing attempts, using strong passwords, and understanding basic email encryption can protect sensitive information.

Internet Usage

- **Web Browsers (e.g., Chrome, Firefox, Safari):** Understand how to navigate websites, bookmark essential pages, and adjust settings for a personalized browsing experience.

- **Search Engines:** Using platforms like Google or Bing efficiently, understanding Boolean search operators, and discerning reliable sources from unreliable ones is essential in today's information age.

- **Online Collaboration Tools:** Platforms like Zoom, Microsoft Teams, or Google Meet have become central to remote work and online collaboration. Knowing how to schedule, join, and participate in virtual meetings is pivotal.

Cloud Storage and Collaboration

Platforms like Google Drive, Dropbox, and Microsoft OneDrive allow users to store files online, granting access from any device and facilitating easy collaboration.

- **Storing & Organizing:** Uploading files, creating folders, and organizing data.

- **Sharing & Collaboration:** Providing access to others, understanding permission levels, and using real-time collaboration features.

Cybersecurity Basics: In a digitally connected world, cybersecurity is of paramount importance. Recognizing threats, understanding the importance of regular software updates, and using trusted antivirus software can safeguard crucial data.

Continuous Learning and Adaptability: With technology continually evolving, staying updated with the latest tools and platforms is crucial. Regular training, online tutorials, and workshops can assist in staying ahead of the curve.

Computer literacy is a linchpin for daily operations for any aspirant or professional in the civil services. In a world that leans heavily on digital communication and data management, understanding these fundamental tools and practices isn't just advantageous—it's imperative. The technological landscape will continue to change, but one is better prepared to evolve alongside it with a solid foundation. As we venture further into the digital age, the confluence of technology and governance will only become more pronounced, making computer literacy an undeniably essential competency for future civil servants.

Administrative Procedures: Filing, Scheduling, and Office Protocols

Whether at the federal or state level, a government office thrives on organization. It is the scaffolding upon which the vast edifice of the administrative process stands. From the filing systems that help categorize decades of information to the scheduling tools that ensure no two meetings clash, managerial procedures form the linchpin of government functioning. This section aims to comprehensively understand these procedures, focusing on filing, scheduling, and essential office protocols.

THE IMPORTANCE OF ADMINISTRATIVE PROCEDURES

Administrative procedures serve as the backbone of an organized office. They create an efficient, structured, and systematic environment where tasks are performed seamlessly, ensuring no data is lost and activities are synchronized.

Filing: More than Just Storage

- **Physical Filing Systems:** Even in the digital age, hard-copy documents play a role. Understanding how to organize files in cabinets, using color-coded tabs, alphabetical or chronological systems, and creating a document inventory can speed up retrieval.

- **Digital Filing Systems:** Computers and cloud storage have revolutionized filing. Creating folders, sub-folders, and naming conventions for files ensures that digital data is always at your fingertips. Regular backups, using trusted storage solutions, and understanding access permissions are crucial.

- **Document Retention & Disposal:** Not all documents need to be kept indefinitely. Understanding which documents to retain, the duration, and the secure disposal methods for outdated or unnecessary documents can protect sensitive information and declutter the workspace.

Scheduling: The Art of Time Management

- **Using Digital Tools:** Platforms like Microsoft Outlook or Google Calendar allow appointments, meetings, and reminders to be set with notifications. They also enable shared calendars for team visibility.

- **Prioritizing Tasks:** Not all tasks hold the same weight. Prioritizing daily tasks, meetings, and projects can lead to better productivity.

- **Allocating Buffer Time:** Understanding that back-to-back meetings can reduce efficiency is essential. Allocating buffer times ensures preparation and offers brief rest periods.

- **Recurring Reviews:** Weekly or monthly reviews of schedules can identify patterns, routine tasks, or meetings that can be optimized or combined.

Office Protocols: The Unwritten Rules

- **Communication:** Clear and effective communication, whether via email, memos, or face-to-face conversations, ensures everyone is on the same page.

- **Hierarchy & Reporting:** Recognizing the chain of command, understanding who reports to whom, and respecting orders can ensure smooth communication and decision-making.

- **Confidentiality:** Many government documents are sensitive. Knowing what information to share, with whom, and how to securely store such documents is a crucial protocol.

- **Dress Code:** Many government offices have a dress code reflecting the decorum and professionalism of public service. Adhering to it shows respect for the institution and the role one plays.

- **Attendance & Punctuality:** Regular attendance and punctuality are not just markers of professionalism but also ensure the workflow is uninterrupted.

The Role of Technology in Administrative Procedures

- **Digital Management Systems:** Platforms like Enterprise Resource Planning (ERP) or Customer Relationship Management (CRM) software can assist in managing vast amounts of data and inter-departmental activities.

- **Automated Scheduling Tools:** Tools allowing automated scheduling, task assignment, or even AI-driven priority setting can enhance efficiency.

- **Digital Communication Platforms:** Slack, Microsoft Teams, or other intra-office communication platforms can streamline communication, file sharing, and collaborative efforts.

Continuous Training & Adaptability

Administrative procedures, while foundational, are not static. As technology evolves, so do best practices in filing, scheduling, and office protocols. Regular training sessions, workshops, or seminars can ensure that all staff members are up-to-date with the latest advancements.

In the intricate machinery of government offices, administrative procedures are the gears and cogs that keep everything running smoothly. From the tactile feel of a well-organized filing cabinet to the ease of a digital calendar reminder, these procedures are integral to the daily life of a civil servant. With technology continuously reshaping the landscape, a keen understanding paired with an adaptability to learn and evolve becomes the hallmark of an effective and efficient administrator.

MATHEMATICAL ABILITIES

Often seen as the universal language, mathematics has imprinted its mark on various aspects of human civilization. From engineering marvels to financial structures, its influence is undeniable. When it comes to civil service, mathematical abilities help perform basic job tasks and serve as foundational skills, enabling civil servants to analyze data, budget resources, and make informed decisions. This chapter will delve into the significance of mathematical abilities within civil service and provide insights into its various facets.

Relevance in the Civil Service

Mathematics isn't reserved for scientists or engineers; it's deeply embedded in the daily operations of government agencies. Mathematical competencies are vital, whether allocating funds for a community project, analyzing census data, or determining taxation rates. They allow for:

- **Precision & Accuracy:** Ensuring that financial reports are accurate, tax calculations are correct, or census data is adequately analyzed is crucial. A foundational understanding of math ensures precision in these tasks.

- **Data Analysis:** Government agencies are inundated with vast volumes of data. From crime statistics to environmental data, dissecting and understanding these numbers is indispensable.

- **Budgeting & Resource Allocation:** Government budgets determine the functioning of various departments and projects. Mathematical skills ensure the efficient distribution of resources, preventing wastages and shortfalls.

Core Mathematical Skills for Civil Servants

- **Arithmetic:** Basic arithmetic is foundational. Adding, subtracting, multiplying, and dividing are skills used daily, whether it's in processing applications, calculating fees, or managing finances.

- **Statistics:** Given the vast amounts of data that government agencies deal with, understanding mean, median, mode, variance, and other statistical concepts can help in data interpretation and decision-making.

- **Algebra:** Civil servants sometimes need to solve for unknown variables, especially in roles that require financial or logistical planning.

- **Geometry and Measurement:** For tasks that involve spatial reasoning, understanding areas, volumes, and distances can be critical. This is especially true for urban planning, environmental agencies, or infrastructure development roles.

Enhancing Mathematical Abilities

- **Regular Practice:** Like any other skill, common practice can sharpen one's mathematical abilities. Engaging in tasks that involve calculations or even solving puzzles can be beneficial.

- **Use of Software Tools:** With the advent of technology, myriad software tools are designed to aid mathematical calculations. Leveraging technology can enhance accuracy from spreadsheet software to specialized financial planning tools.

- **Continuous Learning:** Enrolling in refresher courses or attending workshops can help you stay updated with the latest mathematical tools and techniques.

Mathematical abilities may not always take center stage in the civil service's vast landscape, but they invariably form a part of the backdrop. The precision of arithmetic, the analytical nature of statistics, and the problem-solving aspects of algebra are all tools in the civil servant's toolkit. As society continues to evolve and the nature of challenges facing the government becomes more complex, the integration of mathematics with technology and analytical thinking will only grow in importance. Whether directly or indirectly, every civil servant will, at some point in their career, rely on their mathematical abilities to serve their community better.

Arithmetic: Basic Operations, Percentages, and Ratios

Basic Operations: The foundation of any mathematical computation rests upon four pillars: addition, subtraction, multiplication, and division. For civil servants, proficiency in these basic operations is paramount, especially when dealing with voluminous datasets, financial transactions, and statistical computations.

Addition

Application in Civil Service: The addition is used in aggregating multiple figures, be it a summation of the budget from various departments, accumulation of votes during an election, or acquisition of survey data across multiple categories.

Example: A civil service officer in the Department of Finance may need to add up revenue from various sources—such as taxes, levies, fines, and licenses—to get the total income of the state.

Subtraction

Application in Civil Service: Subtraction offers insights into differences or gaps. It could be utilized to determine budget deficits, calculate the difference between projected and actual outcomes, or understand the gap between policy intent and real impact.

Example: An urban planner might use subtraction to determine how much more infrastructure investment is needed by taking the target infrastructure value and subtracting the current infrastructure value.

Multiplication

Application in Civil Service: Multiplication, an extension of repeated addition, finds use in extrapolating data, determining total costs, or computing area and volume measurements.

Example: A civil servant in the public health department might use multiplication to calculate the total dosage of a vaccine required by multiplying the dose per person with the number of individuals to be vaccinated.

Division

Application in Civil Service: Division plays a role in the distribution of resources, calculating average values, or determining rates. It gives a perspective on how a whole can be divided into parts.

Example: A housing department officer might utilize division to calculate the average space per person in a housing facility by dividing the total area by the number of occupants.

Percentages

Understanding Percentages: Percentages are fractional values expressed in terms of a hundred. They provide a standardized way to compare quantities.

Application in Civil Service: Percentages are pivotal in policy making and analysis. They convey data changes over time, comparative data across departments or regions, and the effectiveness of policies.

Example: In the context of education, a civil servant might analyze the percentage change in high school graduation rates over a decade to assess the impact of an educational reform policy.

Interpreting Percentage Increases and Decreases

Often, officers need to interpret percentage values in reports, especially when comparing year-on-year data or understanding growth or decline trends.

Example: If the unemployment rate dropped from 10% to 7%, it signifies a 3% absolute decrease but a 30% relative decrease in unemployment figures.

RATIOS

Grasping Ratios: Ratios illustrate the relationship between two quantities. They provide a comparative perspective and are a critical resource allocation and analysis tool.

Application in Civil Service: Ratios help civil servants make comparative evaluations, optimize resource distribution, and conduct demographic studies, among other tasks.

Example: A transportation department might look at the ratio of public transport users to private vehicle users to strategize on improving public transportation systems.

Real-world Ratio Implications: Ratios often have real-world policy implications. For instance, a high student-to-teacher ratio in schools might indicate overcrowded classrooms, necessitating hiring more teachers or constructing more schools.

While the arithmetic tools of basic operations, percentages, and ratios seem elementary, their application in the civil service is vast and critical. They aid in data interpretation, policy formulation, resource allocation, and impact assessment. For a civil servant, these aren't just mathematical concepts but are indispensable tools for effective governance and administration. With the sheer volume and complexity of data that government bodies handle, a clear understanding of these arithmetic principles ensures accuracy, clarity, and judicious decision-making.

Data Interpretation: Reading Charts, Graphs, and Tables

The dynamic realm of civil service thrives on information. Information must be quickly and efficiently deciphered to make timely decisions. In this environment, data visualization tools like charts, graphs, and tables bridge the gap between raw data and actionable insights. While numerical proficiency remains a cornerstone of data interpretation, the ability to glean pertinent information from these visual tools is equally, if not more, crucial.

Understanding the Need for Data Visualization

Speed and Efficiency: In the time-pressed world of civil services, a bar chart can provide insights much quicker than a 100-row table. Visualization tools compress vast data into easily digestible visuals, enabling prompt decision-making.

Recognizing Trends and Patterns: Graphs and charts render patterns, anomalies, and trends discernible. For instance, a line graph can effortlessly convey the ebb and flow of unemployment rates over decades, something a spreadsheet might struggle to do as efficiently as possible.

Making Comparisons: Pie charts, column graphs, and even tables allow officials to juxtapose figures, departments, regions, or years, laying the groundwork for analytical deliberation.

Delving into the Tools: Charts, Graphs, and Tables

Charts

- **Pie Charts:** They represent parts of a whole. A pie chart can reveal the distribution of the federal budget among various departments or how a particular state's demographics break down by ethnicity.
- **Bar and Column Charts:** Ideal for comparison. For instance, comparing the annual budget allocations over years or the GDP growth of different states.
- **Donut Charts:** A variant of pie charts, often used to represent multiple categories within a more extensive variety.

Graphs

- **Line Graphs:** Perfect for showcasing trends over time. They can depict the growth trajectory of public transportation users or the decline in crime rates.
- **Area Graphs:** Similar to line graphs, shade the area under the line, emphasizing volume. They can effectively demonstrate the accumulation of budget surpluses or deficits over time.
- **Scatter Plots:** Depict correlations. For instance, to discern if there's a correlation between education spending and literacy rates in various counties.

Tables

Tables, the silent workhorses of data presentation, structure data in rows and columns. They're invaluable for presenting raw figures' specific details and facilitating a deep dive into the data.

Strategies for Effective Interpretation

Identify the Key Message: Every visualization encapsulates a story or a primary message. Recognizing this narrative is the first step in data interpretation. What is the overarching theme or trend is the graph or table attempting to convey?

Context is Crucial: Data without context can be misleading. Ensure you know the background, data source, and the methodologies used in its collection and presentation.

Examine Data Points and Intervals: Always pay attention to scales, especially on graphs. A misinterpretation of scales can lead to grossly incorrect conclusions. Likewise, be cautious of manipulated axes, which exaggerate or diminish apparent trends.

Cross-reference with Other Data: Never rely on a single chart or graph. Always look for additional data or sources to corroborate the information presented.

Pitfalls and Common Errors

Confirmation Bias: Often, we see what we want to see. When interpreting data, it's imperative to remain objective and not just look for patterns reinforcing our pre-existing beliefs.

Overgeneralization: While a pie chart might show that 40% of a city's population uses public transport, it doesn't mean that every district in the town has the same statistic.

Misleading Visualizations: Not all visualizations are created with honesty. Be wary of charts or graphs without labeled axes, use inconsistent scales, or employ dramatic visuals to represent minimal differences.

The Future of Data Interpretation

With the advent of artificial intelligence and big data, the future will likely usher in even more complex data visualizations. Tools like heat maps, 3D graphs, and interactive dashboards will demand advanced interpretative skills. Moreover, virtual reality might reshape how we interact with and perceive data, necessitating an evolved skill set for civil servants.

In civil service, data is the compass and map, guiding decisions and shaping policies. Charts, graphs, and tables are the tools that distill this vast data into actionable insights. Mastery in data interpretation isn't just an asset; it's a necessity. As data burgeon in complexity, the aptitude to decipher, analyze, and act upon it will remain at the heart of effective governance.

Problem-Solving: Applying Mathematical Concepts to Real-World Scenarios

Problem-solving stands as a cornerstone of effective governance and efficient administration in the realm of civil services. It involves addressing multifaceted issues with a toolkit of logic, analysis, and, often, mathematical concepts. Applying these principles to real-world scenarios is more than mere computation; it's about drawing connections, making informed decisions, and achieving optimized solutions.

The Intrinsic Link: Mathematics and Decision-Making

Analytical Foundations: At its core, mathematics equips individuals with a structured way of thinking. Civil servants employ mathematical frameworks to dissect problems, analyze their components, and craft viable solutions, whether dealing with budgets, demographic trends, or infrastructural projects.

Predictive Capabilities: Mathematics allows for informed forecasting. With robust data and mathematical models, decision-makers can anticipate outcomes, gauge potential risks, and make proactive choices.

Key Mathematical Concepts in Problem-Solving

Statistics and Probability: Understanding and interpreting statistical data is crucial in policy-making. It involves:

1. Evaluating population demographics to guide social programs.
2. Analyzing crime statistics to bolster law enforcement strategies.
3. Gauging the probability of events, like natural disasters, to improve preparedness.

Algebraic Thinking

Algebra is about more than just solving for 'x.' In administrative contexts, it can involve:

1. Calculating projected costs for municipal projects.
2. Assessing the financial impact of policy changes.
3. Estimating resource allocation based on variable factors.

Geometric and Spatial Reasoning

Understanding spatial relationships is paramount in city planning, transportation, and infrastructure development. This includes:

1. Optimizing road networks or public transport routes.
2. Calculating areas or volumes for construction projects.
3. Designing efficient layouts for public spaces.

Real-world Scenarios and Mathematical Application

Budget Allocations: When distributing a state's annual budget across various departments, officials often lean on mathematical models to ensure optimal allocation. This might involve analyzing past expenditure data, forecasting future needs, and using linear programming to maximize benefits under constraints.

Disaster Response: Mathematical models can help predict the impact of natural disasters, allowing officials to allocate resources efficiently. For instance, using fluid dynamics to anticipate flood paths or employing statistical models to predict the spread and impact of wildfires.

Urban Planning: Mathematics aids city planners in optimizing public transportation routes, anticipating traffic flow, design green spaces, and ensuring equitable access to public amenities. Tools like graph theory can help in understanding and improving network connectivity.

The Art of Translating Mathematical Solutions to Actions: While mathematics can provide answers, translating these into actionable policies is an art. It requires:

- **Communication Skills:** It's vital to convey complex mathematical conclusions in a manner understandable to stakeholders and the general public.

- **Ethical Considerations:** Just because a solution is mathematically optimal doesn't mean it's ethically correct. Balancing mathematical conclusions with ethical considerations is paramount.

- **Flexibility:** Real-world scenarios are dynamic. Civil servants must be adaptable and willing to recalibrate solutions as situations evolve.

The Pitfalls: Challenges and Limitations

Over-reliance on Models: Mathematical models, while powerful, are based on assumptions. Over-relying on them without considering external factors can lead to flawed decisions.

Misinterpretation: A misread graph, a misunderstood statistical metric, or an overlooked variable can significantly skew conclusions. Continuous training and skill enhancement are crucial to prevent such missteps.

Ethical Quandaries: Sometimes, mathematical outcomes can present ethical dilemmas, especially when they clash with social equity or justice considerations. Balancing the two is an ongoing challenge.

Future Horizons: The Evolving Landscape: As data becomes more intricate and computational tools more advanced, the role of mathematics in problem-solving will only grow. Anticipating this, civil services must:

1. Invest in training programs that merge mathematical theory with practical application.

2. Collaborate with academia and industry to harness the latest mathematical tools and methodologies.

3. Encourage a culture of continuous learning and adaptability.

Mathematics, in the context of civil services, transcends mere numbers. It's a framework, a methodology, and a critical tool in the decision-making arsenal. By effectively harnessing and applying mathematical concepts to real-world scenarios, civil servants can craft both efficient and impactful solutions, driving forward the engine of governance with precision and foresight.

VERBAL SKILLS

In civil services, where communication forms the bedrock of effective governance, the mastery of verbal skills cannot be overstated. Whether articulating policies, negotiating with stakeholders, or addressing the public, conveying thoughts and ideas clearly and persuasively is crucial.

The Multifaceted Nature of Verbal Skills: Verbal skills encompass more than just the words we utter. It's a symbiosis of vocabulary, tone, context, intent, and pauses between words. In the context of civil services:

- Articulation becomes essential when explaining intricate policies or laws to the public.
- Persuasion is pivotal in negotiating terms, rallying support for initiatives, or calming tensions during crises.
- Active listening, a nuanced facet of verbal skills, is vital when taking feedback, understanding grievances, or participating in discussions.

Verbal Skills in Daily Civil Service Activities: Day-to-day activities in civil services are rife with instances where verbal skills come to the fore:

- **Meetings & Deliberations:** Civil servants frequently engage in meetings, requiring them to express ideas succinctly, argue convincingly, and listen actively.
- **Public Addresses:** Whether addressing a community gathering or facing the media, civil servants must be articulate, clear, and confident.
- **Document Reviews:** Though primarily written, understanding the nuance and tone of documents (like legal texts) requires sharp verbal comprehension.

The Ripple Effect of Effective Verbal Communication: The benefits of honed verbal skills in civil services are manifold:

- **Building Trust:** Clear communication fosters trust. When constituents understand policies and motivations, they will likely support and adhere to them.
- **Efficiency:** Effective verbal communication can streamline processes, minimize misunderstandings, and expedite decisions.
- **Collaboration:** Inter-departmental projects thrive on clear communication. With verbal skills, collaboration becomes smoother, leading to better outcomes.

Nurturing Verbal Skills: Recognizing the importance of verbal skills, aspiring and serving civil servants can adopt several strategies to enhance them:

- **Training & Workshops:** Participating in oratory workshops, debate clubs, and public speaking courses can hone articulation and persuasion abilities.
- **Active Listening Practice:** This can be fostered through group discussions where the focus is as much on absorbing others' viewpoints as expressing one's own.
- **Reading Aloud:** It might sound elementary, but reading newspapers or reports aloud can refine pronunciation, enhance vocabulary, and instill confidence.

In an information overload era, verbal communication is a beacon of clarity. For civil servants, it's not just about speaking; it's about making every word count, ensuring every message resonates, and weaving a tapestry of trust, clarity, and collaboration through the power of words. As the adage goes, "The pen is mightier than the sword," but in civil services, the spoken word can often prove mightier still with its immediacy and impact.

Reading Comprehension: Understanding and Interpreting Written Information

In an information-saturated era, the ability to comprehend and interpret written text has become a paramount skill. This is especially true for individuals in civil services who routinely engage with diverse forms of documentation, from intricate legal documents to public communications. Reading comprehension goes beyond just decoding words. It involves understanding context, discerning the main idea, identifying nuances, and drawing inferences.

Understanding Reading Comprehension: Reading comprehension is the ability to understand, remember, and communicate information from written text. Several components contribute to comprehensive reading:

- **Literal Understanding:** Grasping the direct information, facts, and details presented.
- **Inferential Understanding:** Interpreting implied information or drawing conclusions based on the text.
- **Evaluative Understanding:** Analyzing the text's quality, credibility, and relevance.
- **Applicative Understanding:** Using the information from the text in real-life scenarios.

Importance of Reading Comprehension in Civil Services: For civil servants, the stakes for reading comprehension are considerably high:

- **Decision Making:** Many decisions involve understanding extensive reports, studies, or documents. Misinterpreting these can lead to flawed conclusions.
- **Public Communication:** Misreading or misunderstanding can lead to misinformation, causing unnecessary panic or confusion.
- **Legal and Policy Interpretation:** Inaccuracies in interpreting laws or policies can have significant ramifications, from legal disputes to policy failures.

Factors Influencing Reading Comprehension: Several factors play a role in determining an individual's reading comprehension ability:

- **Vocabulary Knowledge:** A vital vocabulary aids in understanding intricate texts without constant reference to a dictionary.
- **Prior Knowledge:** Familiarity with the subject matter often leads to better comprehension.
- **Purpose of Reading:** Comprehension differs when reading for leisure, research, or critical analysis.
- **Cognitive Abilities:** Attention span, memory, and analytical skills contribute significantly to comprehension levels.

Strategies to Enhance Reading Comprehension: Enhancing reading comprehension is not an overnight feat but involves consistent efforts:

- **Active Reading:** Engage with the text by underlining, noting in margins, and asking questions.
- **Summarizing:** After a section, pause to recap the main points mentally or in writing.
- **Visualizing:** Create mental images for scenarios described in the text.
- **Questioning:** Ask questions before, during, and after reading to gauge understanding and anticipation.
- **Context Clues:** Use surrounding sentences or paragraphs to decipher the meaning of challenging words or concepts.

Challenges in Reading Comprehension: While reading comprehension is crucial, it isn't devoid of challenges:

- **Ambiguity:** Some texts, primarily legal or philosophical, can be ambiguous.
- **Volume:** The sheer volume of information can be overwhelming, leading to skimming rather than detailed reading.
- **Bias and Misinformation:** In today's age of "fake news," distinguishing credible sources from unreliable ones is vital.

Technological Aids in Reading Comprehension: With advancements in technology, several tools are available to aid comprehension:

- **Digital Highlighters** allow users to highlight and annotate directly on digital documents.
- **Reading Apps:** Apps that adjust font size, background color, and spacing can enhance reading comfort and comprehension.
- **Summary Tools:** Some software can provide concise summaries of lengthy documents, although they should be used judiciously.

Practical Applications in Civil Services: In the sphere of civil services, reading comprehension is continually applied:

- **Policy Drafting:** Understanding international agreements or prior policies is foundational to drafting new ones.
- **Legal Cases:** Comprehending legal documents, judgments, and related literature is crucial for case preparations.
- **Public Feedback:** Civil servants often gauge public sentiment through written feedback, requiring keen comprehension.

Continuous Development: Like any skill, reading comprehension requires regular practice and refinement. Engaging with diverse reading materials, challenging oneself with intricate texts, and regularly practicing comprehension exercises can lead to steady improvements.

Reading comprehension stands as a sentinel at the gates of knowledge. For civil servants, it's not just about reading words but understanding the tapestry of ideas, emotions, facts, and inferences those words create. It's about sifting through volumes of information and distilling essence, ensuring that decisions are informed, policies are robust, and the public is aptly served. Reading comprehension is the guiding light in the intricate maze of written information, ensuring clarity, precision, and understanding.

Grammar & Vocabulary: Standard American English Rules and Usage

Grammar and vocabulary form the bedrock of effective communication. In the context of civil services, an in-depth understanding of Standard American English (SAE) is paramount. Such experience ensures clear, concise, and error-free communication in written reports, public announcements, or interpersonal dialogues. Dive in as we unravel the intricacies of SAE rules and its rich vocabulary tapestry.

Understanding Standard American English (SAE): Standard American English refers to standardizing English language usage in the United States. While regional dialects and colloquialisms abound, SAE provides a unified linguistic framework, especially vital in formal contexts.

1. **Grammar:** The structured system governing the arrangement of words and phrases.
2. **Vocabulary:** The collection of words and their meanings.

Fundamental Grammatical Principles of SAE

1. **Sentence Structure:** English sentences typically follow a subject-verb-object pattern. For example, "She (subject) reads (verb) the book (object)."

2. **Tense and Aspect:** SAE recognizes three primary tenses (past, present, future) and four aspects (simple, progressive, perfect, perfect-progressive), creating a matrix of twelve tense-aspect combinations.

3. **Pronouns:** These replace nouns and must agree in number and gender with those they return.

4. **Modifiers:** Adjectives and adverbs modify nouns and verbs, respectively. Their placement in a sentence is crucial for clarity.

5. **Prepositions:** These indicate spatial, temporal, or logical relationships. Common prepositions include "in," "on," "under," and "between."

Richness of American English Vocabulary: American English boasts a vast and dynamic vocabulary enriched by the following:

- **Etymology:** Words derived from Latin, Greek, French, and native languages.

- **Synonyms:** Multiple words with similar meanings, e.g., "big," "large," or "huge."

- **Antonyms:** Words with opposite meanings, e.g., "hot" vs. "cold."

- **Homonyms:** Words that sound alike but have different meanings, e.g., "bare" vs. "bear."

Vocabulary Building for Civil Services: Given the formal and expansive nature of civil services communications, building a robust vocabulary is essential:

- **Contextual Learning:** Understand words in context. Reading official documents, journals, or newspapers can provide exposure to formal vocabulary.

- **Word Lists:** Lists focusing on formal and academic words can be beneficial.

- **Root Words:** Recognizing Latin and Greek roots can aid in deciphering unfamiliar words.

- **Thesaurus Usage:** Regularly using a thesaurus can provide synonyms and enhance word variety in communication.

Common Grammatical Challenges in SAE

- **Subject-Verb Agreement:** Ensuring the subject and verb in a sentence agree in number.

- **Misplaced Modifiers:** Avoid ambiguity by correctly placing modifying words or phrases.

- **Parallel Structure:** Ensuring consistent grammatical form in lists or comparisons.

Nuances of Vocabulary Usage in Civil Services

- **Formality:** Choosing words that match the formal tone of civil services documentation.

- **Precision:** Using specific terms over vague ones for clarity.

- **Avoiding Jargon:** Opt for universally understood terms unless you communicate with a specialized audience.

Resources for Enhancing Grammar and Vocabulary

- **Grammar Handbooks:** These provide comprehensive overviews of grammar rules.
- **Online Platforms:** Websites like Grammarly or the Purdue OWL offer grammar checks and explanations.
- **Vocabulary Apps:** Apps like Anki or Quizlet allow users to create custom flashcards for vocabulary expansion.
- **Writing Workshops:** Regular participation can hone both grammatical accuracy and vocabulary usage.

Practical Applications in Civil Services

- **Policy Drafting:** Unambiguous language ensures policies are universally understood and correctly implemented.
- **Legal Documents:** Precision in language usage can prevent potential legal misunderstandings or disputes.
- **Public Communication:** Well-constructed, grammatically accurate statements foster trust and clarity among the public.

Mastering the rules of Standard American English grammar and its expansive vocabulary is more than just an academic exercise. For civil servants, it's a commitment to clarity, precision, and effective communication. The adage goes, "It's not just what you say, but how you say it." In the corridors of public service, this rings especially true, as the nuances of grammar and the richness of vocabulary play pivotal roles in bridging the divide between intent and understanding.

WRITING AND SPELLING: PRODUCING CLEAR, ERROR-FREE WRITTEN CONTENT

Effective communication is not merely a skill but a necessity in civil services. The documents you create, the emails you send, and the reports you compile reflect your capabilities and the organization you represent. The importance of impeccable writing and spelling in this sector cannot be overstated. This chapter offers a deep dive into crafting straightforward, error-free written content, emphasizing fundamental principles, pitfalls to avoid, and resources to fine-tune your writing and spelling skills.

The Importance of Writing in Civil Services

In civil services, you're often responsible for drafting essential documents such as policy proposals, memos, and public notices. Clarity, consistency, and error-free writing are non-negotiables. Any oversight could lead to misunderstandings, legal complications, and loss of public trust.

Critical Components of Effective Writing

1. **Structure:** A well-structured writing has a clear introduction, body, and conclusion. Each paragraph should represent a single idea or concept.
2. **Clarity:** Avoid jargon, complex sentence structures, and any elements confining the reader.
3. **Conciseness:** Be direct. Remove any superfluous words or phrases.
4. **Tone:** The tone should be appropriate for the target audience. In most civil service contexts, a formal tone is advisable.

Common Spelling Pitfalls and How to Avoid Them

- **Homophones:** Words like "their," "there," and "they're" are often mixed up. Context is crucial in choosing the correct word.
- **Prefixes/Suffixes:** Words like "irresistible" and "unmanageable" can trip you up. Always double-check the spelling of such words.
- **Double Consonants:** Words like "accommodate" and "commitment" often pose challenges. Practice is the best way to master these.

Strategies for Effective Writing

- **Drafting:** Always create a draft first. The first draft is just that—a breeze. It needn't be perfect.
- **Editing:** Once the draft is complete, review it for clarity, coherence, and grammatical errors. Spell-check tools are helpful, but only rely on them partially.
- **Peer Review:** Having another set of eyes look at your work can offer invaluable insights.
- **Final Review:** Before submitting or publishing, read through your work one last time, preferably aloud, to catch any lingering errors.

Resources for Writing and Spelling Improvement

- **Grammarly:** This tool provides real-time spelling and grammar checks.
- **Thesaurus:** It's an excellent resource for diversifying your vocabulary and enhancing your writing.
- **Style Guides:** Manuals like the Chicago Manual of Style or the Associated Press (AP) Stylebook offer comprehensive writing guidelines.
- **Writing Workshops:** These are particularly useful for improving both the creative and technical aspects of your writing.

The essence of effective communication in the civil services lies in your ability to convey complex information in the most straightforward manner possible. This isn't a skill developed overnight but cultivated over time. Given the significant implications of errors in this field, continuous learning and practice are imperative. From honing your grammar to expanding your vocabulary and mastering the art of spelling, each aspect is crucial in ensuring your written communication is up to the mark.

Essay Writing: Structuring and Producing Coherent, Focused Essays

Essay writing is crucial in various professions, including civil services. Essays are used to present information, argue a point, or share a perspective in a structured manner. A well-crafted piece demonstrates the writer's ability to think critically, structure thoughts, and communicate effectively. This section will delve into the essay writing process, emphasizing the importance of structure, coherence, and focus.

The Essence of a Good Essay

Before we venture into the mechanics of essay writing, it's essential to understand what makes an essay stand out:

- **Clarity:** The central idea should be evident.
- **Cohesion:** The paper should flow logically from one point to the next.
- **Concision:** Every word should have a purpose.
- **Conviction:** Arguments should be presented confidently and backed with evidence.

The Process of Essay Writing

- **Understanding the Prompt:** Ensure you know what the question or prompt asks before writing. Identify key terms and the type of response expected (argumentative, descriptive, etc.)
- **Research:** Gather information from reliable sources to support your essay. Take notes, highlighting essential facts, quotes, or data.
- **Brainstorming:** List the main ideas you want to include, drawing connections between them.
- **Developing a Thesis Statement:** This one or two-sentence statement encapsulates your essay's main point or argument.
- **Outlining:** Structure your essay by determining how you'll introduce your topic, present your arguments, and conclude your essay.

Structuring the Essay

- *Hook:* Start with an engaging sentence to grab the reader's attention.
- *Background Information:* Provide context for your topic.
- *Thesis Statement:* Present your main argument or point.
- *Body Paragraphs (typically three or more)*
- *Topic Sentence:* Introduces the main idea of the paragraph.
- *Supporting Details:* Facts, quotes, or data supporting your point.
- *Explanation:* Elaborate on how the supporting details validate your argument.
- *Transition:* Use transitional words or sentences to guide the reader to the next paragraph.

Conclusion

- *Restate the Thesis:* Recap your main argument without merely repeating it.
- *Summarize Key Points:* Briefly revisit the main ideas presented in the body.
- *Closing Thoughts:* End with a thought-provoking statement or a call to action.

Coherence and Flow

Achieving coherence is about ensuring that your ideas link seamlessly. Some techniques include:

1. **Transitional Phrases:** Words like "however," "furthermore," and "as a result" guide readers through your essay.

2.

3. **Consistent Tense and Point of View:** Shifting tenses or perspectives can confuse readers.

4. **Parallel Structure:** This involves using consistent grammatical forms. For instance, "reading, writing, and speaking" rather than "reading, writing, and speaking."

Revision and Proofreading

No essay is perfect in its first draft:

1. **Revision:** Review your essay, refining arguments and ensuring clarity and coherence. Look out for areas that could be more specific or redundant.

2. **Proofreading:** This is your final check for grammar, spelling, and punctuation errors.

Essay writing is a systematic process that requires planning, organization, and revision. While the ability to craft a compelling essay comes with practice, understanding the fundamental principles of structure, coherence, and focus lays the foundation for improvement. For those in civil service, mastering essay writing is not just an academic exercise but a tool for effective communication, influencing policy, and advocating for change.

QUESTIONS AND ANSWERS

GENERAL KNOWLEDGE

Q: What are the founding documents of the United States?

A: The founding documents of the U.S. are the Declaration of Independence, the Constitution, and the Bill of Rights. These documents established the nation's independence, governmental framework, and fundamental rights.

Q: Who was Harriet Tubman?

A: Harriet Tubman was an abolitionist and conductor on the Underground Railroad, helping hundreds of enslaved individuals escape to freedom in the 19th century. Later, she also played roles as a scout and nurse during the Civil War.

Q: What was the significance of the Louisiana Purchase?

A: The Louisiana Purchase in 1803 doubled the size of the United States, acquiring vast territories west of the Mississippi River from France and opening up the continent for westward expansion.

Q: Describe the significance of the Emancipation Proclamation.

A: Issued by Abraham Lincoln in 1863, the Emancipation Proclamation declared the freedom of all enslaved individuals in Confederate-held territory, shifting the Civil War's focus towards liberty and equality.

Q: Who were the "Suffragettes"?

A: The "Suffragettes" were women's rights activists in the early 20th century who advocated for and eventually achieved the right to vote for women through the 19th Amendment in 1920.

Q: What are the three branches of the U.S. government?

A: The three branches are the Executive (headed by the President), the Legislative (consisting of the Senate and House of Representatives), and the Judicial (led by the Supreme Court).

Q: Describe the principle of "checks and balances."

A: "Checks and balances" is a system in which each branch of government can limit or check the power of the other branches, preventing any single branch from gaining too much authority.

Q: What is the central role of the Executive branch?

A: The Executive Branch enforces federal laws, directs national defense and foreign policy, and conducts diplomacy with other nations.

Q: How does the Constitution allocate powers between federal and state governments?

A: The Constitution uses the principles of "federalism," granting certain powers exclusively to the federal government, reserving some for states, and allowing some to be shared.

Q: What is the Bill of Rights?

A: The Bill of Rights comprises the first ten amendments to the U.S. Constitution, ensuring specific rights and liberties to individuals and states.

Q: What was the significance of the Paris Agreement?

A: The Paris Agreement, signed in 2016, is an international treaty to address climate change by limiting global temperature rises. The U.S. initially joined, later withdrew and then rejoined the agreement.

Q: Describe the impact of the COVID-19 pandemic in the U.S.

A: The COVID-19 pandemic drastically affected the U.S. with significant loss of life, economic downturns, shifts to remote work, and pressing discussions on public health policies.

Q: How has social media influenced U.S. politics in recent years?

A: Social media has reshaped political engagement, enabling direct communication between officials and the public, amplifying grassroots movements, and playing roles in election campaigns and policy debates.

Q: What are some current discussions on immigration reform in the U.S.?

A: Current immigration discussions focus on issues like DACA, border security measures, pathways to citizenship, and refugee resettlement policies.

Q: Why was the Black Lives Matter movement significant?

A: The Black Lives Matter movement, initiated in 2013, gained widespread attention for advocating against systemic racism and violence towards Black individuals, significantly influencing national conversations on race and justice.

Q: Who were the principal authors of the Federalist Papers?

A: The Federalist Papers were penned by James Madison, Alexander Hamilton, and John Jay. These documents advocated for ratifying the U.S. Constitution, outlining the benefits of a strong central government.

Q: What event led to the start of the Civil War?

A: The Civil War was precipitated by numerous factors, but the immediate event was the Confederate attack on Fort Sumter in South Carolina in April 1861.

Q: Who is Susan B. Anthony?

A: Susan B. Anthony was a leading activist in the women's suffrage movement in the U.S. She played a pivotal role in pushing women's voting rights.

Q: Describe the Great Migration.

A: The Great Migration refers to relocating over six million African Americans from the rural South to the North, Midwest, and West cities from 1916 to 1970. They sought better economic opportunities and to escape racial segregation and discrimination.

Q: What was the purpose of the Marshall Plan?

A: Post World War II, the Marshall Plan aimed to rebuild and stabilize European economies to prevent the spread of communism by providing significant U.S. financial and technical assistance.

Q: What role does the Vice President play in the Senate?

A: The Vice President of the U.S. serves as the President of the Senate and can cast a tie-breaking vote if the Senate is evenly split on a decision.

Q: How is a U.S. Supreme Court Justice appointed?

A: A U.S. Supreme Court Justice is nominated by the sitting U.S. President and must be confirmed by the Senate following hearings and a vote.

Q: What are implied powers in the context of the U.S. Constitution?

A: Implied powers refer to powers not explicitly stated in the Constitution but inferred from the "Necessary and Proper" or "Elastic" clause, allowing the federal government to carry out enumerated powers effectively.

Q: What is the 10th Amendment about?

A: The 10th Amendment states that any powers not delegated to the federal government nor prohibited to the states are reserved for the states or the people.

Q: How do states' rights differ from federal rights?

A: While federal rights are powers and responsibilities given to the national government by the Constitution, states' rights refer to all powers not explicitly granted to the federal government or denied to states.

Q: What is net neutrality, and why is it debated?

A: Net neutrality is the principle that internet service providers should treat all data equally without favoring or blocking specific sites or content. It's debated because of concerns over free access to the internet versus provider discretion and potential regulation.

Q: What has been the U.S. stance on the World Health Organization (WHO) recently?

A: As of my last update in 2021, the U.S. had announced its intention to leave the WHO in 2020 but later rejoined under a new administration in 2021, emphasizing global health collaboration.

Q: What is the Green New Deal?

A: The Green New Deal is a proposed economic stimulus package that addresses climate change and economic inequality, emphasizing renewable energy, infrastructure development, and job creation.

Q: How did the opioid crisis start in the U.S.?

A: The opioid crisis began in the late 1990s when pharmaceutical companies reassured medical professionals that opioid pain relievers weren't addictive, leading to widespread prescription, misuse, and a surge in opioid-related overdose deaths.

Q: What was the significance of the #MeToo movement?

A: The #MeToo movement, gaining momentum in 2017, highlighted the prevalence of sexual harassment and assault, particularly in the workplace, leading to global conversations, policy changes, and the accountability of several high-profile individuals.

Q: What was the significance of the Louisiana Purchase?

A: The Louisiana Purchase in 1803 doubled the size of the United States, providing vast territories for westward expansion, and was acquired from France for $15 million, marking a pivotal moment in American territorial growth.

Q: Who was Harriet Tubman, and why is she remembered?

A: Harriet Tubman was a former enslaved African American who became a conductor on the Underground Railroad, leading hundreds to freedom. She's remembered for her bravery and dedication to ending slavery.

Q: What impact did the Industrial Revolution have on the U.S.?

A: The Industrial Revolution transformed the U.S. from an agrarian society into an industrialized nation, leading to urbanization, technological advancements, changes in labor patterns, and significant economic growth.

Q: What is the Monroe Doctrine?

A: The Monroe Doctrine, established in 1823, declared that the Western Hemisphere was off-limits to new European colonization and that the U.S. would not interfere in the internal affairs of European nations.

Q: Who were the "Rough Riders"?

A: The "Rough Riders" were a volunteer cavalry regiment led by Theodore Roosevelt during the Spanish-American War in 1898. They are most famously known for their charge up San Juan Hill in Cuba.

Q: What are the key responsibilities of the House of Representatives?

A: The House of Representatives is responsible for originating revenue bills, impeaching federal officials, and electing the President in the event of an Electoral College tie, among other duties.

Q: How does the system of checks and balances work?

A: The system ensures that every branch of government becomes sufficiently robust. For example, while Congress creates laws, the President can veto them, and the Supreme Court can declare laws unconstitutional. Thus, each branch can check the powers of the others.

Q: What are the primary rights protected by the First Amendment?

A: The First Amendment to the U.S. Constitution safeguards five primary rights: freedom of speech, religion, press, assembly, and the right to petition the government.

Q: How does the Electoral College function?

A: The Electoral College is a body of electors chosen by each state to vote for the President and Vice President. While most states have a winner-takes-all system, the candidate with the majority of electoral votes, not necessarily popular votes, wins the presidency.

Q: What is the significance of the 19th Amendment?

A: The 19th Amendment, ratified in 1920, granted women the right to vote, marking a significant expansion of suffrage in the United States.

Q: How has climate change impacted U.S. policies in the 21st century?

A: Climate change has progressively influenced U.S. policies, leading to international accords like the Paris Agreement, increased regulations on emissions, and discussions on renewable energy and sustainability to mitigate environmental impacts.

Q: How did the Black Lives Matter movement impact societal discourse?

A: The Black Lives Matter movement heightened awareness about systemic racism and police violence, leading to nationwide protests, changes in local policing policies, and broader discussions on racial equity and justice.

Q: How did the COVID-19 pandemic influence U.S. healthcare and economic policies?

A: The pandemic underscored healthcare system vulnerabilities, leading to increased funding for public health, vaccine development, and stimulus packages to support affected businesses and individuals during economic downturns.

Q: What were the U.S.-China trade tensions about in the late 2010s?

A: These tensions revolved around trade imbalances, intellectual property theft, and tariffs. Both nations implemented several rounds of tariffs on each other's goods, leading to global economic implications and discussions on trade practices.

Q: What's the significance of the DACA program in U.S. immigration policy?

A: Deferred Action for Childhood Arrivals (DACA) is a program introduced in 2012, granting temporary protection from deportation and work permits to eligible undocumented immigrants brought to the U.S. as children, highlighting ongoing debates on immigration reform.

OFFICE SKILLS

Q: What's the primary function of spreadsheet software like Microsoft Excel?

A: It's used for organizing, analyzing, and storing data in tabular form, facilitating calculations, graphing, and data analysis.

Q: How do you ensure an email contains a virus-free attachment?

A: Use antivirus software to scan attachments before opening and avoid opening attachments from unknown or suspicious sources.

Q: What's the significance of browser cookies?

A: Cookies store user data to enhance the website browsing experience by remembering user preferences and tracking site visits.

Q: Name a popular tool for video conferencing.

A: Zoom, Microsoft Teams, and Skype are among the popular choices for video conferencing.

Q: Why is it important to regularly update software applications?

A: Regular updates often fix security vulnerabilities, improve functionality, and introduce new features.

Q: How do alphabetical filing systems function?

A: Items are organized alphabetically by name, topic, or specific criteria, ensuring easy and quick retrieval.

Q: What's the purpose of a calendar scheduling tool?

A: It helps in planning, tracking, and managing appointments, meetings, and tasks efficiently.

Q: Why is confidentiality crucial in office settings?

A: It ensures sensitive information remains protected, preserving company integrity client trust, and complying with legal requirements.

Q: Describe the "inbox-zero" approach.

A: It's a productivity strategy that aims to keep the email inbox empty or near-empty by regularly processing and organizing emails.

Q: What's the importance of a clear office protocol?

A: Clear protocols provide standardized procedures, ensuring efficiency, clarity in roles, and smooth operation of daily tasks.

Q: What is the primary role of spreadsheet software in office environments?

A: Spreadsheet software facilitates the organization, analysis, and storage of data in tabular form. Using such software, users can perform myriad tasks, including complex mathematical calculations, data visualization through charts and graphs, and managing financial records, thus streamlining numerous office tasks.

Q: How can one ensure an email attachment is safe to open?

A: Before opening any attachment, it's essential to have updated antivirus software to scan it. Furthermore, being vigilant by not opening attachments from unknown or suspicious sources and checking the file extension for anomalies can add layers of safety.

Q: Why do web browsers utilize cookies, and how do they impact the user experience?

A: Cookies are small data packets stored by browsers to remember a user's website activity or preferences. They enhance the user experience by saving login credentials, preserving session data, and personalizing webpage content based on past visits.

Q: In office communications, how have video conferencing tools revolutionized meetings?

A: Video conferencing tools have bridged geographical barriers, enabling real-time face-to-face interaction between teams, clients, and stakeholders from anywhere in the world. This has fostered improved collaboration, reduced travel costs, and allowed for more flexible work environments.

Q: Why is regularly updating software applications crucial for productivity and security?

A: Keeping software up-to-date is paramount because updates often address security vulnerabilities, enhance performance, fix bugs, and introduce new features, ensuring the system remains secure and functions optimally.

Q: How does an efficient filing system enhance office productivity?

A: An organized filing system ensures quick retrieval and storage of documents, minimizes misplacement risks, and streamlines work processes. Efficient filing can save time, reduce frustration, and enhance office efficiency.

Q: What advantages do digital calendar tools bring to scheduling and time management?

A: Digital calendar tools provide real-time updates, reminders, and synchronization across devices. They help avoid scheduling conflicts, allocate time efficiently, and enable seamless collaboration by showing availability slots and integrating with other office tools.

Q: How does maintaining confidentiality in office settings impact a business's reputation?

A: Upholding confidentiality is essential for preserving the trust of clients, partners, and employees. Breaches can lead to legal repercussions, loss of business, and damage to the company's reputation, making confidentiality practices paramount.

Q: How does practicing good phone etiquette influence customer perceptions?

A: Proper phone etiquette, which includes polite greetings, attentive listening, and clear communication, ensures that customers feel valued, respected, and understood, leading to positive perceptions of trust and fostering stronger client relationships.

Q: Why is it essential for customer service representatives to engage in active listening during interactions?

A: Active listening ensures a comprehensive understanding of the customer's concerns, demonstrating empathy and respect. It not only aids in providing accurate solutions but also builds trust and enhances customer satisfaction.

Q: What strategies can be employed to handle challenging or irate customers over the phone?

A: Handling challenging customers requires patience, empathy, and effective communication. It's crucial to remain calm, listen actively, apologize when necessary, and offer feasible solutions. Sometimes, letting the customer vent can de-escalate the situation, allowing for productive dialogue.

Q: In office administration, why is it essential to have standardized procedures?

A: Standardized procedures ensure consistency, clarity, and efficiency. They provide a clear roadmap for tasks, reducing errors, streamlining training processes, and ensuring everyone works harmoniously towards organizational goals.

Q: What potential risks are associated with mishandling sensitive information in an office setting?

A: Mishandling sensitive data can lead to breaches of confidentiality, legal repercussions, financial losses, damage to the company's reputation, and loss of trust among clients and stakeholders.

Q: How has integrating Customer Relationship Management (CRM) systems transformed customer service?

A: CRM systems centralize customer data, providing a holistic view of client interactions. This aids in personalizing service, predicting customer needs, streamlining communication, and fostering long-term relationships by ensuring every interaction is informed and meaningful.

Q: How do office protocols regarding email communications enhance professionalism and efficiency?

A: Setting clear email protocols, such as appropriate subject lines, timely responses, and avoiding "reply-all" unless necessary, ensures efficient communication. It reduces clutter, enhances clarity, and fosters a professional image for the organization.

Q: Why must office staff be versed in various software tools beyond word processors and spreadsheets?

A: Diverse software tools cater to varied office tasks, from project management to graphic design. Being proficient in various instruments ensures flexibility, enhances productivity, and allows staff to tackle a broader spectrum of jobs efficiently.

Q: In the context of customer service, how has the advent of chatbots influenced public inquiries?

A: Chatbots provide instant responses to common inquiries, enhancing customer experience by reducing wait times. While they streamline initial interactions, human intervention remains crucial for complex issues, balancing efficiency and personalized service.

Q: How do regular backups and cloud storage solutions contribute to effective office management?

A: Regular backups and cloud storage ensure data safety and accessibility. They mitigate risks associated with data loss due to hardware failures or cyber-attacks and allow for seamless access from various locations, enhancing flexibility and collaboration.

Q: Why is it essential to have a protocol for managing incoming and outgoing communications in an office setting?

A: A defined protocol ensures that all communications are tracked, organized, and addressed timely. It avoids miscommunications, provides essential messages that don't fall through the cracks, and maintains a professional and responsive business image.

Q: How do digital tools and platforms impact office protocols and customer service in the modern age?

A: Digital tools have revolutionized office dynamics. They've introduced efficiency, flexibility, and scalability from virtual meetings to AI-driven customer interactions. While they've streamlined many processes, the human touch remains irreplaceable in fostering genuine relationships and handling nuanced situations.

Q: What role do task management tools play in modern offices?

A: Task management tools help teams prioritize and track the progress of individual tasks or larger projects. They foster collaboration, improve delegation efficiency, and provide visual insights into workflow dynamics, ultimately boosting productivity and meeting deadlines.

Q: How do virtual collaboration platforms impact remote work?

A: Virtual collaboration platforms enable real-time communication and document-sharing among remote teams. They help bridge geographical barriers, ensuring team members remain connected, engaged, and productive regardless of physical location.

Q: Why is knowledge of cybersecurity best practices crucial for all office employees?

A: Every employee can be a potential vulnerability or a line of defense. Familiarity with cybersecurity best practices safeguards the organization's sensitive information from threats, ensuring data integrity and protecting against financial and reputational risks.

Q: How does good email etiquette contribute to effective communication?

A: Good email etiquette, which encompasses clarity, brevity, and respect, ensures messages are effectively conveyed and understood. It also avoids misinterpretations and fosters professional relationships both internally and with external partners or clients.

Q: What's the significance of ergonomic office setups?

A: Ergonomic setups optimize comfort and reduce the risk of work-related injuries. They enhance productivity by reducing strain and fatigue and are crucial in promoting employees' long-term health and well-being.

Q: In the digital age, how important is it for offices to maintain a paper trail?

A: While digital records have become predominant, maintaining a paper trail can still be crucial for redundancy, legal requirements, or specific operational needs. It provides a tangible backup in case of digital failures or cybersecurity threats.

Q: How do customer feedback mechanisms influence office protocols and services?

A: Customer feedback provides direct insights into the efficacy of office protocols and services. It highlights areas of improvement, validating successful strategies and offering a roadmap for modifications to serve client needs better.

Q: Why is time management a critical skill for office professionals?

A: Time management ensures optimal utilization of the workday. It aids in meeting deadlines, prioritizing tasks effectively, reducing stress, and balancing work responsibilities and personal time.

Q: How does integrating AI in office tools impact administrative tasks?

AI streamlines administrative tasks by automating repetitive processes, providing predictive analytics, and enhancing accuracy. It saves time and offers valuable insights, driving more intelligent decision-making.

Q: How essential is multitasking in office environments, and what are its pros and cons?

A: Multitasking can boost productivity when handling simple tasks simultaneously. However, it can reduce the quality of work and increase errors when juggling complex tasks. It's essential to discern when to multitask and when to focus singularly for optimal efficiency.

Q: In the context of customer service, how have social media platforms changed the landscape?

A: Social media has transformed customer service by providing a platform for immediate feedback, reviews, and direct communication. Businesses can address grievances, promote transparency, and build brand loyalty through timely and personalized responses.

Q: How do regular training sessions enhance office productivity and skill sets?

A: Regular training keeps employees updated with industry trends, tools, and best practices. It enhances skill sets, boosts morale, fosters innovation, and ensures the team is equipped to tackle evolving challenges efficiently.

Q: What is the significance of backup and disaster recovery plans in offices?

A: Such plans ensure business continuity in the face of unforeseen events like data breaches, natural disasters, or system failures. They protect valuable data, minimize operational disruptions, and safeguard a company's reputation.

Q: How can offices effectively manage distractions to ensure optimal productivity?

A: Effective strategies include setting clear communication protocols, using productivity tools to minimize digital distractions, designating quiet zones, scheduling regular breaks, and fostering a culture that values focus and efficiency.

Q: What is the role of document management systems (DMS) in modern offices?

A: DMS centralizes electronic document storage, retrieval, and tracking. It enhances collaboration, ensures version control, facilitates access permissions, and streamlines workflows, improving efficiency and data security.

Q: Why are soft skills vital in office settings, like empathy and communication?

A: Soft skills foster positive workplace relationships, facilitate effective teamwork, and enhance customer interactions. They're pivotal in navigating challenges, resolving conflicts, and ensuring a harmonious, productive work environment.

Q: How has the proliferation of mobile devices impacted office communication?

A: Mobile devices offer on-the-go communication, making real-time collaboration and instant updates feasible regardless of location. While they've introduced flexibility, they also necessitate clear usage protocols to maintain work-life boundaries and data security.

Q: What's the role of analytics tools in enhancing office operations?

A: Analytics tools provide insights into business processes, pinpointing inefficiencies and areas of improvement. They enable data-driven decision-making, allowing businesses to optimize strategies, forecast trends, and maximize returns on investment.

Q: How have video conferencing tools reshaped office meetings and collaborations?

A: Video conferencing enables face-to-face interactions without geographical constraints. It's cost-effective, fosters a sense of connectedness among remote teams, and allows for versatile meeting formats, from large webinars to one-on-one discussions.

Q: What impact do feedback loops, like peer reviews or customer surveys, have on office operations?

A: Feedback loops provide continuous insights into performance, products, or services. They promote accountability, innovation, and a culture of continuous improvement by ensuring that offices remain responsive to internal and external feedback.

Q: Why is cultural competence vital in modern office settings?

A: Cultural competence ensures respectful and effective communication in diverse workplaces. It fosters inclusivity, reduces misunderstandings, enhances global collaborations, and contributes to a broader perspective and creativity in problem-solving.

Q: How does effective inventory management impact office efficiency?

A: Effective inventory management ensures the timely availability of essential resources and equipment, preventing workflow disruptions. It also aids in budget management, reducing wastage, and ensuring that resources are optimally utilized.

Q: What role does cloud computing play in modern office operations?

A: Cloud computing offers scalable, flexible, cost-effective data storage solutions. It facilitates real-time collaboration, remote access to resources, seamless software updates, and enhanced data security through encrypted backups and disaster recovery options.

Q: In terms of customer service, how important is active listening?

A: Active listening is pivotal to ensuring customers feel heard and valued. It aids in accurately understanding their needs or grievances, leading to more effective problem resolution and fostering trust and loyalty.

Q: What are the benefits of regular team-building exercises in an office setting?

A: Team-building exercises enhance collaboration, boost morale, and improve communication. They help resolve interpersonal conflicts, foster community, and increase productivity and job satisfaction.

Q: How do content management systems (CMS) aid office operations?

A: CMS streamlines digital content creation, management, and publishing. They facilitate collaboration, ensure content consistency, and allow non-technical users to update web content easily, providing timely and cohesive digital communications.

Q: How essential is it for office staff to be familiar with data privacy regulations?

A: With increasing data breaches and stringent regulations, it's vital. Familiarity ensures compliance, protects customer and business data, and prevents legal repercussions and reputational damage.

Q: In what ways do conflict resolution skills impact office dynamics?

A: Effective conflict resolution fosters a positive work environment, reduces disruptions, and ensures that disagreements become opportunities for growth and understanding rather than sources of prolonged tension.

Q: How have project management tools evolved office workflows?

A: These tools offer a centralized task allocation, progress tracking, and resource management platform. They've made workflows more transparent, streamlined communication, ensured timely project delivery, and enhanced team accountability.

Q: Why is adaptability a crucial trait for modern office professionals?

A: The fast-paced evolution of technology and global dynamics requires professionals to be adaptable. This trait ensures they can swiftly learn new tools, navigate changes, and contribute positively to evolving business strategies and challenges.

MATHEMATICAL ABILITIES

Q: How are the basic operations of arithmetic foundational to advanced mathematical concepts?

A: Basic arithmetic operations form the cornerstone of advanced math. They're essential for understanding and building upon more complex topics, ensuring a solid foundation for algebra, calculus, and other higher-level mathematical disciplines.

Q: Why are percentages often used in financial contexts?

A: Percentages offer a standardized way to represent proportions, making comparisons more intuitive. They help understand profit margins, interest rates, and investment returns in finance, offering insights that guide decision-making.

Q: How are ratios different from fractions?

A: While both represent relationships between two numbers, fractions denote parts of a whole, whereas ratios show a relative magnitude between two quantities, often used in contexts like recipes or scale models.

Q: What's the significance of bar graphs in data representation?

A: Bar graphs visually represent data using rectangular bars, making it easier to compare different categories or track changes over time, aiding in quick analysis and comprehension of information.

Q: Why are pie charts particularly effective for showing parts of a whole?

A: Pie charts divide a circle into segments proportional to data values, offering a visual representation of each category's share relative to the whole, making it intuitive to understand distribution or composition.

Q: How do scatter plots aid in identifying trends or relationships between variables?

A: Scatter plots display individual data points on a two-dimensional plane, helping identify patterns, correlations, or anomalies between two variables facilitating predictive analysis and hypothesis testing.

Q: In what scenarios is problem-solving through math especially vital?

A: Mathematical problem-solving is crucial in fields like engineering, economics, physics, and architecture, where real-world challenges require quantitative analysis, modeling, and solutions derived from mathematical principles.

Q: How does one calculate the percentage increase or decrease between two values?

A: Subtract the initial value from the final deal, then divide by the initial value. Multiply by 100 to get the percentage change. This helps assess growth, profit margins, or any relative change effectively.

Q: Why is data interpretation essential in today's data-driven world?

A: In our information-rich age, the ability to interpret and analyze data helps in making informed decisions, spotting trends, and devising effective strategies in fields ranging from business to healthcare.

Q: How do histograms differ from bar graphs?

A: While both are visual representations, histograms group data into ranges or intervals, showcasing frequency distributions, whereas bar graphs represent categorical data with spaces between bars, comparing individual data points or groups.

Q: How are mathematical models used in predicting real-world phenomena?

A: Mathematical models utilize equations and data to simulate and predict real-world scenarios, such as weather patterns, stock market movements, or population growth, providing insights to guide actions or strategies.

Q: What's the importance of understanding compound interest in financial planning?

A: Compound interest considers the principal amount and accumulated interest. Recognizing its exponential growth helps make informed investment decisions and understand the long-term effects of debts or loans.

Q: How can line graphs effectively track progress or changes over time?

A: Line graphs display data points connected by lines, visually illustrating trends, fluctuations, and progress over time, making them ideal for time series data like stock prices, sales figures, or temperature readings.

Q: How are mathematical simulations used in industries?

A: Simulations employ mathematical models to recreate complex real-world processes, enabling industries like aviation, medicine, and manufacturing to test scenarios, optimize performance, or train personnel in risk-free environments.

Q: What role does arithmetic play in everyday life?

A: Arithmetic is foundational to daily tasks, from budgeting, cooking, and shopping to more advanced professional applications in engineering, finance, and research, underscoring its universal relevance.

Q: Why are tables often used alongside graphical data representation?

A: Tables provide detailed numerical data, offering precision and context that complements visual graphs. They allow for a comprehensive understanding of information, balancing detail with visual insight.

Q: How do mathematical concepts aid in strategic decision-making?

A: Mathematical concepts provide quantitative analysis, forecasting, and optimization tools. They offer objective insights, enhancing the accuracy and efficacy of strategic decisions in business, research, and beyond.

Q: What's the significance of understanding conversion rates in business?

A: Conversion rates, often expressed as percentages, measure the effectiveness of strategies, from marketing campaigns to sales pitches. Understanding them helps businesses optimize efforts, allocate resources, and drive growth.

Q: How do box plots provide insights into data distribution?

A: Box plots visually display data's central tendency, spread, and potential outliers, providing a snapshot of its distribution, which aids in understanding variability, skewness, and the overall data landscape.

Q: Why is it essential to have strong problem-solving skills in professions like engineering or finance?

A: These professions face complex, often unprecedented challenges. Mathematical problem-solving offers systematic, logical tools to analyze, model, and address these challenges, ensuring efficient, optimal solutions.

Q: How do you calculate the average of a set of numbers?

A: Add together all the values in the set and divide by the number of values. Averages, or means, offer a centralized value that provides insights into a data set's general trend or characteristic.

Q: Why are trend lines useful in scatter plots?

A: Trend lines, often linear, help deduce the general direction or relationship between variables in a scatter plot. They aid in making predictions, understanding correlations, and providing a summarized view of data patterns.

Q: How are probability and statistics applied in real-world scenarios?

A: These disciplines aid in risk assessment, forecasting, and decision-making. For instance, insurers use them to set premiums, while businesses apply them for market analysis, quality control, and predictive modeling.

Q: What is the role of ratios in financial analysis?

A: Ratios, like debt-to-equity or current ratios, offer insights into a company's financial health, performance, and stability. They allow standardized comparisons across firms and sectors and guide investment and operational decisions.

Q: How does one interpret a pie chart with various segment sizes?

A: Each pie chart segment represents a category's proportion to the whole. More significant segments indicate higher values or ratios, helping viewers quickly assess and compare the relative significance of each type.

Q: How are mathematical algorithms transforming the tech industry?

A: Algorithms rooted in mathematical principles power innovations like machine learning, artificial intelligence, and data analytics. They drive tech advancements, from personalized recommendations to autonomous vehicles and intelligent technologies.

Q: Why is it vital for students to develop a strong foundation in arithmetic?

A: A robust arithmetic foundation ensures students grasp more advanced topics with ease, fostering logical thinking, problem-solving aptitude, and a broader understanding of the world's quantitative aspects.

Q: How do area and bar charts differ in representing data?

A: While both track changes over time, bar charts use individual bars to represent values, whereas area charts shade the region between the data line and the axis, emphasizing volume or quantity and showing cumulative effects.

Q: In what ways do mathematical models influence economic forecasting?

A: Mathematical models analyze historical data, economic indicators, and market dynamics to predict future economic trends. They aid policymakers, investors, and businesses in planning, strategy formulation, and risk mitigation.

Q: How do fractions play a role in real-world scenarios like cooking or construction?

A: Fractions help quantify portions less than a whole, like recipe ingredients or construction blueprint measurements. They ensure precision, consistency, and desired outcomes in tasks that require accurate partitioning.

Q: How are line charts useful in stock market analysis?

A: Line charts visually track stock price movements, offering insights into trends, historical performance, and potential future trajectories. They're fundamental for traders and investors in decision-making.

Q: Why is problem-solving a sought-after skill in job markets?

A: Problem-solving indicates a candidate's ability to approach challenges logically, innovate solutions, and adapt to changing scenarios, making it valuable across professions and industries.

Q: How can one use percentages to compare the growth of two companies?

A: Percentages standardize growth rates, allowing for objective comparisons regardless of company size. By comparing growth percentages, one can assess which company is expanding more rapidly relative to its size.

Q: How does data interpretation play a role in scientific research?

A: Data interpretation allows scientists to derive meaningful insights from experimental results, validate hypotheses, identify patterns, and contribute to knowledge advancement in their respective fields.

Q: What mathematical tools assist in optimizing business operations?

A: Tools like linear programming, statistical analysis, and forecasting models help businesses optimize resource allocation, streamline processes, enhance profitability, and predict market dynamics.

Q: How do tables aid in summarizing vast amounts of data?

A: Tables organize data into rows and columns, enabling quick referencing, comparisons, and pattern identification. They provide clarity, structure, and a condensed view of extensive information.

Q: Why is it crucial to understand decimals when dealing with currencies?

A: Decimals allow for precise representation of values less than one, which is essential when dealing with monetary units like cents in dollars, ensuring accurate financial calculations and transactions.

Q: How do 3D graphs provide added dimensions to data visualization?

A: 3D graphs incorporate an additional axis, enabling the representation of three variables simultaneously. They offer a comprehensive view of data landscapes, aiding in multivariate analysis and interpretation.

Q: Why is mathematical logic foundational in computer programming?

A: Programming involves creating sequences of instructions. Mathematical logic aids in structuring these sequences efficiently, ensuring accurate, optimized outcomes, and forms the backbone of algorithms and computational tasks.

Q: How are ratios used in analyzing business profitability?

A: Ratios like return on investment or profit margin offer insights into how effectively a business utilizes resources to generate profit. They provide benchmarks for performance assessment and guide strategic decisions.

Q: How do histograms aid in understanding frequency distributions?

A: Histograms visually represent data frequency across intervals, helping identify data concentrations, variations, and distribution patterns, which are essential for statistical analysis and inference.

Q: What role does geometry play in architectural design?

A: Geometry aids architects in spatial understanding, ensuring structural integrity, aesthetics, and functional design. It's instrumental in creating blueprints, 3D modeling, and actual construction.

Q: How do companies leverage data visualization in business strategies?

A: Data visualization transforms raw data into understandable formats, helping stakeholders identify trends, make informed decisions, and devise strategies based on actionable insights.

Q: How are quadratic equations relevant in real-world scenarios?

A: Quadratic equations, representing parabolic relationships, arise in various scenarios, from projectile motion in physics to profit maximization in business, making them fundamental in modeling and analysis.

Q: How can one differentiate between mean, median, and mode?

A: The mean is the average, the median is the middle value when data is ordered, and the mode is the most frequent value. Together, they provide insights into data's central tendency and distribution.

Q: Why are Venn diagrams helpful in set theory and logic?

A: Venn diagrams visually represent relationships between sets, showcasing intersections, unions, and differences. They provide a clear, intuitive understanding of complex set relationships and logical propositions.

Q: How do businesses use mathematical forecasting in supply chain management?

A: Mathematical forecasting analyzes historical data and trends to predict future demand. This aids businesses in inventory management, resource allocation, and ensuring timely product availability.

Q: What importance do decimals hold in scientific measurements?

A: Decimals provide precision in scientific measurements, ensuring accurate readings, data recording, and subsequent analyses. They're fundamental in fields that require exactness, like chemistry, physics, and biology.

Q: Why are mathematical models pivotal in environmental studies?

A: These models simulate ecological processes, predict climate changes, and assess human impact. They guide conservation strategies, policy-making, and sustainable development efforts.

Q: How do businesses leverage ratios in market analysis?

A: Price-to-earnings or current ratios offer insights into market dynamics, company valuation, and operational efficiency. Analysts use them to compare companies, assess investment viability, and guide business strategies.

VERBAL SKILLS

Q: Why is reading comprehension a crucial skill in academia?

A: It enables students to understand, interpret, and critically evaluate written information, laying a foundation for informed discussions, research, and knowledge application.

Q: How do context clues aid in understanding unfamiliar vocabulary?

A: Context clues from surrounding text provide hints about an unfamiliar word's meaning, helping readers deduce its significance without external reference.

Q: Why is active voice generally preferred over passive voice in writing?

A: Active voice makes writing direct, clearer, and more engaging by emphasizing the action's doer, while passive voice can sometimes obscure the subject or make sentences longer.

Q: What's the significance of a thesis statement in an essay?

A: A thesis statement presents the essay's central argument or purpose, guiding its structure and offering readers a clear focus and understanding of the content's direction.

Q: How do transition words enhance the flow of a written piece?

A: Transition words bridge ideas, ensuring seamless movement between sentences and paragraphs, enhancing coherence and readability.

Q: Why is it crucial to understand subject-verb agreement in English grammar?

A: Subject-verb agreement ensures consistency and clarity in sentences, preventing confusion and making statements grammatically correct.

Q: How does brainstorming benefit the essay writing process?

A: Brainstorming allows writers to generate, explore, and organize ideas, ensuring a well-rounded, structured, and engaging essay.

Q: Why is proofreading an essential step in writing?

A: Proofreading detects and corrects errors in grammar, spelling, and punctuation, ensuring the final content is polished, professional, and error-free.

Q: How can one enhance their vocabulary consistently?

A: Engaging with diverse reading materials, using new words in writing and speech, and employing tools like flashcards or vocabulary apps can foster vocabulary growth.

Q: Why are concise sentences often more effective than wordy ones?

A: Concise sentences deliver information directly and clearly, improving comprehension and keeping readers engaged.

Q: How does an essay's introduction set the tone for the entire piece?

A: The introduction grabs readers' attention, introduces the topic, and presents the thesis, laying the groundwork for the essay's direction and tone.

Q: Why is it essential to vary sentence structure in writing?

A: Varying sentence structures enhance writing rhythm, maintain reader interest, and emphasize key points more effectively.

Q: How do metaphors and similes enrich written content?

A: They introduce vivid imagery and comparisons, making content more relatable, descriptive, and engaging for readers.

Q: What's the difference between "affect" and "effect"?

A: "Effect" typically denotes action (a verb) meaning to influence, while "effect" is usually a noun referring to a change or result.

Q: Why is understanding the target audience crucial in essay writing?

A: Knowing the audience guides content relevance, tone, vocabulary, and depth, ensuring the essay resonates and effectively communicates its message.

Q: How can paraphrasing assist in understanding complex texts?

A: Paraphrasing involves rewording text in one's own words, ensuring a deeper engagement and more precise understanding of the original material.

Q: Why are prepositions important in English grammar?

A: Prepositions indicate relationships between sentence elements, providing context, direction, and clarity to statements.

Q: How does outlining assist in essay writing?

A: Outlining organizes main ideas and supporting details, providing a roadmap for the essay's structure ensuring coherence and comprehensive coverage.

Q: What role do synonyms play in enhancing written content?

A: Synonyms introduce vocabulary variety, preventing redundancy and making content more vibrant and engaging.

Q: Why is understanding tone and mood essential for reading comprehension?

A: Tone and mood influence content interpretation, guiding readers' emotional responses and understanding of the writer's intent.

Q: What's the significance of a conclusion in an essay?

A: Conclusions summarize vital points and reiterate the thesis, offering closure and emphasizing the essay's central message.

Q: Why is active listening essential for effective verbal communication?

A: Active listening ensures complete comprehension, fosters meaningful responses, and strengthens interpersonal relationships.

Q: How does punctuation influence the meaning of sentences?

A: Punctuation guides sentence flow, clarity, and emphasis, directly influencing interpretation and meaning.

Q: How do you differentiate between "its" and "it's"?

A: "Its" is a possessive pronoun denoting ownership, while "it's" is a contraction of "it is" or "it has."

Q: How can writers ensure clarity in their content?

A: Clarity can be achieved by using straightforward language, maintaining focus, structuring content logically, and avoiding ambiguity.

Q: How do idioms enrich language?

A: Idioms introduce cultural nuances and expressions, making language colorful, relatable, and contextually rich.

Q: Why is understanding irony crucial for reading comprehension?

A: Irony involves a contrast between appearance and reality. Recognizing it ensures accurate interpretation and appreciation of deeper textual layers.

Q: How do suffixes and prefixes aid in deducing word meanings?

A: Suffixes and prefixes modify base words, providing hints about their function or meaning and helping readers infer word definitions in context.

Q: What are the benefits of peer review in the writing process?

A: Peer review offers fresh perspectives, constructive feedback, and error detection, refining and enhancing the final piece.

Q: How does repetition function as a rhetorical device in writing?

A: Repetition emphasizes key points, evokes emotions, and reinforces ideas, making content more memorable and impactful.

Q: How do authors employ symbolism in literature?

A: Symbolism uses characters, objects, or events to represent deeper meanings or concepts, enriching narrative layers and evoking thoughtful interpretation.

Q: How does understanding context aid in reading comprehension?

A: Context offers background information, clarifying ambiguities, enriching interpretation, and providing a framework for understanding textual nuances.

Q: Why are adverbs crucial in modifying verbs?

A: Adverbs describe how, when, where, or to what extent an action occurs, offering depth and detail to verbs enhancing sentence clarity.

Q: How can writers avoid clichés in their content?

A: Avoiding clichés involves being aware of overused phrases, seeking original expressions, and ensuring authentic, fresh perspectives in writing.

Q: What role does pacing play in narrative writing?

A: Pacing controls story progression, tension, and reader engagement, determining how quickly events unfold and influencing emotional impact.

Q: Why is consistency in verb tense essential in writing?

A: Consistent verb tense maintains clarity, ensures smooth flow, and prevents reader confusion, upholding narrative continuity.

Q: How can writers improve their spelling skills?

A: Regular reading, practicing writing, using spell-check tools, and employing mnemonic devices can bolster spelling proficiency.

Q: Why are analogies effective in explaining complex concepts?

A: Analogies draw parallels between familiar and unfamiliar ideas, simplifying complexities and fostering clearer understanding.

Q: How can one differentiate between "your" and "you're"?

A: "Your" is a possessive pronoun denoting ownership, while "you're" is a contraction of "you are."

Q: How do writers create tension in narrative essays?

A: Tension arises from conflicts, pacing variations, descriptive language, and unpredictability, keeping readers engaged and invested.

Q: How do conjunctions function in sentence construction?

A: Conjunctions connect words, phrases, or clauses, ensuring coherence, continuity, and logical flow in sentences.

Q: Why are character-driven narratives effective in essays?

A: Character-driven narratives engage readers emotionally, offering relatable experiences and insights and evoking empathy and connection.

Q: How does an understanding of root words benefit vocabulary expansion?

A: Root words are base words to which prefixes and suffixes attach. Knowing them helps deduce the meanings of complex words, aiding vocabulary comprehension and acquisition.

Q: How can freewriting enhance the essay drafting process?

A: Freewriting allows writers to express ideas without restrictions, fostering creativity and generating content that can be refined and structured later.

Q: Why is it important to avoid redundancy in writing?

A: Redundancy can make content repetitive and tedious. Eliminating it ensures concise, engaging, and clear writing.

Q: How do authors use foreshadowing in literature?

A: Foreshadowing offers hints or clues about upcoming events, building anticipation and deepening narrative layers.

Q: Why is it crucial to differentiate between "then" and "then"?

A: "Then" denotes time sequences, while "then" is used for comparisons. Correct usage ensures clarity and grammatical accuracy.

Q: How do writers ensure a balanced argument in essays?

A: A balanced argument presents multiple perspectives, supports claims with evidence, addresses counterarguments, and maintains an unbiased tone.

Q: What role do sensory details play in descriptive writing?

A: Sensory details evoke visual, auditory, tactile, olfactory, and gustatory images, immersing readers in the described scenario and enhancing experience.

Q: How can writers effectively conclude argumentative essays?

A: Effective conclusions restate the thesis, summarize main points, and leave readers with a compelling thought or call to action, solidifying the essay's impact.

PRACTICE TEST

Prepare to challenge yourself with our Practice Test section, designed to simulate real-world testing scenarios across different subjects. Each test has been calibrated to offer a balance of simplicity and complexity, ensuring participants can gauge their proficiency levels. Regularly taking these practice tests can improve comprehension, recall, and examination readiness. So, gear up and measure where you stand with these engaging tests.

GENERAL KNOWLEDGE

1. **Question:** Which of the following documents was primarily concerned with the structure of the U.S. federal government?

   A) The Articles of Confederation

   B) The Magna Carta

   C) The U.S. Constitution

   D) The Declaration of Independence

2. **Question:** Which President served a non-consecutive term?

   A) Ulysses S. Grant

   B) Theodore Roosevelt

   C) Grover Cleveland

   D) John Adams

3. **Question:** The principle that the U.S. federal courts can declare a law unconstitutional is known as:

   A) Judicial Review

   B) Checks and Balances

   C) Federalism

   D) Separation of Powers

4. **Question:** Which significant figure is credited with drafting the Declaration of Independence?

   A) Benjamin Franklin

   B) George Washington

   C) Thomas Jefferson

   D) James Madison

5. **Question:** Does the U.S. Senate have how many members?

   A) 100

   B) 435

   C) 50

   D) 270

6. **Question:** Who was the U.S. president during the Civil War?

   A) Andrew Johnson

   B) James Buchanan

   C) Abraham Lincoln

   D) Thomas Jefferson

7. **Question:** In which year did the U.S. enter World War I?

   A) 1917

   B) 1914

   C) 1920

   D) 1916

8. **Question:** The right of citizens to vote cannot be denied based on gender, as per which amendment?

   A) 19th amendment

   B) 15th amendment

   C) 14th amendment

   D) 21st amendment

9. **Question:** Which body has the power to impeach the President?

   A) The Senate

   B) The House of Representatives

   C) The Supreme Court

   D) The Cabinet

10. **Question:** Who was the first U.S. Secretary of the Treasury?

    A) Thomas Jefferson

    B) John Adams

    C) Alexander Hamilton

    D) James Madison

11. **Question:** The U.S. acquired a significant portion of its western territory through which event?

   A) The Homestead Act

   B) The Gadsden Purchase

   C) The Oregon Trail

   D) The Louisiana Purchase

12. **Question:** Which agency is responsible for U.S. foreign intelligence and counterintelligence?

   A) FBI

   B) CIA

   C) NSA

   D) Homeland Security

13. **Question:** What was the primary cause of the Spanish-American War?

   A) Territory disputes

   B) Trade embargoes

   C) The sinking of the Maine

   D) Alliance obligations

14. **Question:** Which President is best known for his role in the Cuban Missile Crisis?

   A) John F. Kennedy

   B) Richard Nixon

   C) Dwight D. Eisenhower

   D) Lyndon B. Johnson

15. **Question:** Who wrote the majority of the Federalist Papers?

   A) James Madison

   B) John Jay

   C) Alexander Hamilton

   D) Benjamin Franklin

16. **Question:** In which year did the stock market crash, signaling the start of the Great Depression?

   A) 1939

   B) 1929

   C) 1919

   D) 1949

17. Question: Which case confirmed the principle of "separate but equal"?

    A) Marbury v. Madison

    B) Brown v. Board of Education

    C) Plessy v. Ferguson

    D) Roe v. Wade

18. Question: Which Constitutional Amendment abolished slavery in the U.S.?

    A) 13th amendment

    B) 15th amendment

    C) 19th amendment

    D) 14th amendment

19. Question: What is the primary responsibility of the Executive Branch of the U.S. government?

    A) Making laws

    B) Enforcing laws

    C) Interpreting laws

    D) Ratifying treaties

20. Question: Which event was directly responsible for the start of the American Revolutionary War?

    A) The signing of the Declaration of Independence

    B) The Boston Tea Party

    C) The Boston Massacre

    D) Battles of Lexington and Concord

21. Question: Which U.S. state was the last to be admitted to the Union?

    A) Hawaii

    B) Alaska

    C) Arizona

    D) New Mexico

22. Question: Which body is tasked with the power of the purse in the U.S. government?

    A) The Senate

    B) The House of Representatives

    C) The Supreme Court

    D) The Executive Office

23. Question: What does the 4th amendment protect citizens against?

    A) Double jeopardy

    B) Unreasonable searches and seizures

    C) Cruel and unusual punishment

    D) Self-incrimination

24. Question: Which of the following was a significant cause of the War of 1812?

    A) Impressment of American sailors

    B) Taxation without representation

    C) The sinking of the USS Maine

    D) Territorial disputes in the West

25. Question: Which international accord sought to address climate change in the 21st century?

    A) The Geneva Accords

    B) The Paris Agreement

    C) The Helsinki Accords

    D) The Bretton Woods Agreement

26. Question: Who is third in the line of succession for the U.S. presidency?

    A) Secretary of State

    B) Vice President

    C) Speaker of the House

    D) Senate Majority Leader

27. Question: Which landmark case established the principle of judicial review?

    A) Plessy v. Ferguson

    B) Roe v. Wade

    C) Marbury v. Madison

    D) McCulloch v. Maryland

28. Question: What is the total number of voting members in the U.S. House of Representatives?

    A) 100

    B) 435

    C) 538

    D) 365

29. **Question:** What was the primary goal of the Civil Rights Movement in the 1960s?

   A) Abolishing slavery

   B) Women's suffrage

   C) Racial equality and the end of Jim Crow segregation

   D) Native American rights

30. **Question:** Which President signed the Civil Rights Act of 1964 into law?

   A) John F. Kennedy

   B) Lyndon B. Johnson

   C) Richard Nixon

   D) Dwight D. Eisenhower

31. **Question:** Which U.S. President signed the Emancipation Proclamation?

   A) George Washington

   B) Thomas Jefferson

   C) Abraham Lincoln

   D) Andrew Jackson

32. **Question:** What is the primary role of the U.S. Judicial Branch?

   A) Enforce laws

   B) Create laws

   C) Interpret laws

   D) Veto laws

33. **Question:** Who was the principal author of the Declaration of Independence?

   A) Benjamin Franklin

   B) John Adams

   C) Thomas Jefferson

   D) James Madison

34. **Question:** Which amendment to the U.S. Constitution provides freedom of speech?

   A) First

   B) Second

   C) Fourth

   D) Eighth

35. Question: In which decade did the U.S. women gain the right to vote?

    A) 1920s

    B) 1930s

    C) 1940s

    D) 1960s

36. Question: Who is considered the "Father of the Constitution"?

    A) George Washington

    B) Alexander Hamilton

    C) Benjamin Franklin

    D) James Madison

37. Question: What role does the U.S. Senate play in presidential impeachments?

    A) It investigates the charges.

    B) It votes to impeach the President.

    C) It conducts the impeachment trial.

    D) It pardons the President.

38. Question: Which event started the Civil Rights Movement in the 1950s and 1960s?

    A) The assassination of Martin Luther King Jr.

    B) The Montgomery Bus Boycott

    C) The March on Washington

    D) The Voting Rights Act

39. Question: How many branches of government does the U.S. have?

    A) Two

    B) Three

    C) Four

    D) Five

40. Question: Which governing body has the power to declare war?

    A) The President

    B) The Supreme Court

    C) The House of Representatives

    D) The Senate

41. **Question:** Who wrote the Federalist Papers?

   A) Thomas Jefferson and John Adams

   B) Alexander Hamilton, James Madison, and John Jay

   C) Benjamin Franklin and George Washington

   D) Patrick Henry and Samuel Adams

42. **Question:** Which state was the first to secede from the Union leading to the Civil War?

   A) Virginia

   B) Texas

   C) South Carolina

   D) Tennessee

43. **Question:** What is the primary function of the Executive branch?

   A) Interpret laws

   B) Create laws

   C) Enforce laws

   D) Veto laws

44. **Question:** What does the Bill of Rights represent?

   A) A list of presidential powers

   B) The first ten amendments to the U.S. Constitution

   C) A treaty with foreign nations

   D) A bill passed during the Civil War

45. **Question:** Which President was responsible for the New Deal in response to the Great Depression?

   A) Herbert Hoover

   B) Franklin D. Roosevelt

   C) Harry Truman

   D) Woodrow Wilson

46. **Question:** Which Supreme Court case established the principle of judicial review?

   A) Dred Scott v. Sandford

   B) Plessy v. Ferguson

   C) Roe v. Wade

   D) Marbury v. Madison

47.

48. Question: Who serves as the President of the Senate?

    A) The Senate Majority Leader

    B) The Vice President of the United States

    C) The Speaker of the House

    D) The Chief Justice of the Supreme Court

49. Question: Which amendment abolished slavery in the U.S.?

    A) 13th amendment

    B) 14th amendment

    C) 15th amendment

    D) 19th amendment

50. Question: How many justices serve on the U.S. Supreme Court?

    A) 7

    B) 8

    C) 9

    D) 10

51. Question: What is the primary focus of the State of the Union address?

    A) Discussing foreign relations

    B) Announcing presidential candidacies

    C) Updating Congress on national issues and setting an agenda

    D) Celebrating national holidays

OFFICE SKILLS

1. **Question:** Which software is primarily used for creating presentations?

   A) M.S. Word

   B) M.S. Excel

   C) M.S. PowerPoint

   D) M.S. Access

2. **Question:** Which protocol is primarily used to send emails?

   A) HTTP

   B) FTP

   C) SMTP

   D) UDP

3. **Question:** When scheduling meetings, which tool assists in finding a time when all participants are available?

   A) Spell Check

   B) Calendar

   C) File Explorer

   D) Task Manager

4. **Question:** Which file extension typically denotes a compressed file?

   A) .txt

   B) .docx

   C) .zip

   D) .ppt

5. **Question:** In which of these would you store contact information in a structured manner?

   A) Spreadsheet

   B) Presentation

   C) Database

   D) Word document

6. **Question:** If a client expresses dissatisfaction, what's the first thing you should do?

   A) Offer a discount immediately

   B) Interrupt and correct them

   C) Listen actively and empathetically

   D) Transfer them to a supervisor

7. **Question:** Which software can be used to track and manage customer interactions?

   A) CRM

   B) CMS

   C) ERP

   D) IDE

8. **Question:** What's the primary purpose of using BCC in an email?

   A) To send attachments

   B) To hide recipients from each other

   C) To mark the email's importance

   D) To send a carbon copy

9. **Question:** In an office setting, what does VPN stand for?

   A) Virtual Public Network

   B) Variable Procedure Notation

   C) Virtual Private Network

   D) Variable Private Node

10. **Question:** Which of the following is NOT a standard image file format?

    A) .jpeg

    B) .png

    C) .xls

    D) .gif

11. **Question:** What's a primary consideration when scheduling a business call with a client in a different time zone?

    A) The weather in the client's location

    B) Your lunch schedule

    C) The time difference

    D) The phase of the moon

12. **Question:** Which of these is crucial to good phone etiquette when answering a business call?

    A) Using slang to sound friendly

    B) Eating while speaking

    C) Identifying yourself and the organization

    D) Putting the caller on hold immediately

13. Question: What's the primary purpose of a firewall in computer systems?

    A) Speeding up the system

    B) Blocking unauthorized access

    C) Assisting in web design

    D) Data storage

14. Question: When a customer queries about a product or service, what's the best initial action?

    A) Transfer them to another department without explanation

    B) Tell them to check the website

    C) Offer an immediate solution without listening fully

    D) Take time to understand their question or concerns thoroughly

15. Question: Which among the following is NOT a component of M.S. Office Suite?

    A) M.S. Word

    B) M.S. Excel

    C) Adobe Photoshop

    D) M.S. PowerPoint

16. Question: What does the computer term "browser" refer to?

    A) A type of virus

    B) The hard drive

    C) Software used to navigate the internet

    D) RAM storage

17. Question: What does the term "sub-folder" mean in a hierarchical office filing system?

    A) A folder within another folder

    B) A leading directory

    C) The desktop

    D) A software tool

18. Question: If a customer raises their voice on the phone, what's an appropriate response?

    A) Raise your voice in return

    B) Hang up the phone

    C) Remain calm and try to address their concerns

    D) Tell them to call back later

19. Question: Which among the following is a standard software tool for project management?

A) Photoshop

B) Trello

C) Skype

D) WinZip

20. Question: What's essential to ensuring a smooth video conference call?

A) Having a decorative background

B) Stable internet connection

C) Using a lot of emojis

D) Playing music in the background

21. Question: If a document needs to be shared with multiple team members for collaboration, which tool would be most appropriate?

A) Adobe Reader

B) Windows Media Player

C) Google Docs

D) Paint

22. Question: What is the primary role of antivirus software on a computer?

A) Improving graphics

B) Speeding up the CPU

C) Detecting and removing malicious software

D) Assisting with internet browsing

23. Question: In a professional setting, why is it crucial to respond to emails promptly?

A) To free up storage space

B) To maintain professionalism and show respect to the sender

C) Because emails expire after 24 hours

D) To avoid computer viruses

24. Question: What does the term "cloud storage" refer to?

A) Physical storage in a computer's hard drive

B) Saving data in atmospheric clouds

C) Storing data on remote servers accessed via the internet

D) A backup drive

25. Question: What does "CC" in an email context stand for regarding administrative procedures?

   A) Current Client

   B) Computer Communication

   C) Credit Card

   D) Carbon Copy

26. Question: When assisting clients over the phone, why is it helpful to repeat or paraphrase their concerns?

   A) To fill the conversation time

   B) To ensure clarity and show that you've understood their issue

   C) Because it's a standard phone script

   D) To test the client's patience

27. Question: Which application best suits numerical data analysis and presentation in tabular form?

   A) M.S. Word

   B) M.S. Excel

   C) M.S. Paint

   D) M.S. Outlook

28. Question: What does the acronym "FAQ" stand for in customer service?

   A) Fast Answer Queue

   B) Frequent Ask Question

   C) Fully Answered Questions

   D) Frequently Asked Questions

29. Question: When organizing a digital workspace, what is the purpose of creating folders and subfolders?

   A) To increase the computer's speed

   B) To make the screen look more colorful

   C) To organize and categorize files for easy access

   D) To use up more storage space

30. Question: In an office setting, why is it essential to back up digital files and data regularly?

   A) To consume more bandwidth

   B) To increase the workload

   C) To protect against data loss due to unforeseen events or technical issues

   D) Because it's a trendy thing to do

VERBAL SKILLS

1. **Question:** Which of the following is NOT a synonym for 'benevolent'?

   A) Kind-hearted

   B) Malevolent

   C) Generous

   D) Charitable

2. **Question:** In the sentence, "The dog's tail wagged furiously," what part of speech is "furiously"?

   A) Adjective

   B) Adverb

   C) Noun

   D) Verb

3. **Question:** Which of the following words is spelled correctly?

   A) Recieve

   B) Archive

   C) Believe

   D) Deceive

4. **Question:** What is the primary purpose of an introductory paragraph in an essay?

   A) Conclude the essay's argument

   B) List all the sources used

   C) Introduce the topic and provide background

   D) Highlight the main points discussed in the body

5. **Question:** What tense is the verb in this sentence: "She will have finished her assignment by tomorrow"?

   A) Past continuous

   B) Present perfect

   C) Future perfect

   D) Present continuous

6. **Question:** Which sentence is grammatically correct?

   A) Their going to the market today.

   B) They're book is on the table.

   C) There studying for the exam.

   D) They're going to the beach.

7. **Question:** When writing an essay, what should the body primarily contain?

   A) Repetition of the thesis statement

   B) New topics not mentioned in the introduction

   C) Detailed support for the thesis statement

   D) Personal opinions without evidence

8. **Question:** Which word is an antonym for 'arduous'?

   A) Difficult

   B) Demanding

   C) Simple

   D) Strenuous

9. **Question:** Which of the following sentences uses correct punctuation?

   A) Its a sunny day; isn't it?

   B) It's a sunny day, isn't it.

   C) It's a sunny day, isn't it?

   D) Its a sunny day; isn't it.

10. **Question:** The primary goal of a conclusion paragraph in an essay is to:

    A) Introduce a new topic for the following essay

    B) Summarize and reinforce the main points

    C) Provide detailed evidence and examples

    D) Repeat the introduction verbatim

11. **Question:** Which of the following words is an adverb?

    A) Quickly

    B) Quick

    C) Quicken

    D) Quickness

12. **Question:** The phrase "a dime a dozen" means:

    A) Very expensive

    B) Quite rare

    C) Common and of little value

    D) Worth 10 cents

13. Question: Which of these is not a type of pronoun?

A) Adjective

B) Reflexive

C) Possessive

D) Interrogative

14. Question: If an essay topic asks you to "compare and contrast", you should:

A) List all the similarities between the items

B) Explain why one item is superior

C) Discuss both similarities and differences

D) Describe the items without comparing them

15. Question: The word "its" in the sentence "The cat chased its tail" is a:

A) Contraction

B) Verb

C) Possessive pronoun

D) Noun

16. Question: Which of the following sentences correctly uses a semicolon?

A) The cake is delicious; it's chocolate.

B) The cake; is delicious because it's chocolate.

C) The cake is delicious it's chocolate.

D) The cake is; delicious because it's chocolate.

17. Question: A good thesis statement should:

A) Be vague and general

B) Clearly state the main idea or argument

C) Be placed at the end of the essay

D) Avoid taking a stance

18. Question: Which word completes this analogy? "Whisper is to shout as mumble is to _____."

A) Talk

B) Scream

C) Listen

D) Ask

19. **Question:** In the sentence "She is walking to the store," what is the verb phrase?

   A) She is

   B) Is walking

   C) Walking to

   D) Walking to the store

20. **Question:** Which sentence correctly uses "their," "there," and "they're"?

   A) Their going over there to get they're backpacks.

   B) They're going over there to get their backpacks.

   C) Their going over they're to get there backpacks.

   D) There going over their to get they're backpacks.

21. **Question:** Which of the following is an antonym for "benevolent"?

   A) Kind

   B) Generous

   C) Malevolent

   D) Joyful

22. **Question:** In which sentence is the word 'their' used correctly?

   A) Their going to the store.

   B) I love their new song.

   C) Let's go to their house and play.

   D) Their is no reason to worry.

23. **Question:** What is the primary purpose of a thesis statement in an essay?

   A) To provide evidence

   B) To restate the conclusion

   C) To entertain the reader

   D) To present the main idea

24. **Question:** Which of the following sentences is grammatically correct?

   A) She don't like chocolate.

   B) Him and I went to the park.

   C) They're going to they're friends house.

   D) The cats chased their tails.

25. Question: When writing an essay, what should be included in the body paragraphs?

   A) A restatement of the thesis

   B) Background information

   C) Supporting details and evidence

   D) A summary of the main points

26. Question: Which of the following sentences has a spelling mistake?

   A) The desert is scorching during the day.

   B) She wanted to complement his work.

   C) I need to go grocery shopping.

   D) It's raining outside.

27. Question: In the context of reading comprehension, what does 'inference' mean?

   A) Direct information stated in the text

   B) Making predictions based on the title

   C) Drawing a conclusion based on given information

   D) Counting the number of words in the text

28. Question: Which sentence uses punctuation correctly?

   A) She said "Are you coming over tonight."

   B) "Where are you going, John asked.

   C) "How are you feeling?" he inquired.

   D) "It's raining, outside"

29. Question: When writing an essay, the conclusion should primarily:

   A) Introduce a new argument

   B) Directly copy the introduction

   C) Summarize the main points and restate the thesis in a new way

   D) Ask a series of unrelated questions

30. Question: In which sentence is 'too' used correctly?

   A) I am too tired too go out.

   B) Too books are on the table.

   C) She wants too play a game.

   D) The movie was too long for my liking.

31. Question: A piece of writing that primarily aims to persuade the reader is called:

A) A narrative

B) An expository text

C) A descriptive text

D) An argumentative text

32. Question: Which word is spelled correctly?

A) Seperately

B) Definately

C) Accommodate

D) Existance

33. Question: Which sentence correctly uses the word 'its'?

A) The dog wagged its tail.

B) Its raining heavily outside.

C) The cat played with it's toy.

D) Its been a long time.

34. Question: In reading comprehension, 'context clues' are used to:

A) Make the text longer

B) Decorate the text

C) Understand the meaning of an unfamiliar word or phrase

D) Change the meaning of known words

35. Question: Which of the following sentences is in the passive voice?

A) The chef cooked the meal.

B) The chef cooked the meal.

C) She sings a song.

D) He drove the car fast.

36. Question: When analyzing a text, the term 'main idea' refers to:

A) The title of the text

B) The most frequently used word

C) The overall point or message the author is conveying

D) The last sentence in the text

37. Question: Which of the following sentences uses 'whom' correctly?

   A) Whom is going to the store?

   B) To whom should I address the letter?

   C) I don't know whom car this is.

   D) Whom is the best player?

38. Question: What should a writer primarily focus on in the introduction of an essay?

   A) Presenting evidence and data

   B) Discussing minor details

   C) Introducing the main topic and capturing the reader's interest

   D) Giving a detailed conclusion

39. Question: In the sentence, which word is an adjective: "She wore a beautiful blue dress."?

   A) Wore

   B) She

   C) Beautiful

   D) Dress

40. Question: A coherent essay is one that:

   A) Uses complex vocabulary

   B) Is written in multiple languages

   C) Flows logically and is easy to follow

   D) Focuses on multiple unrelated topics

MATHEMATICAL ABILITIES

1. **Q:** What is 12% of 250?

   A) 25

   B) 30

   C) 15

   D) 30

2. **Q:** If a shirt initially costs $50 and is on a 20% sale, what is the discounted price?

   A) $10

   B) $40

   C) $35

   D) $45

3. **Q:** If a car travels 360 miles in 6 hours, what is its average speed?

   A) 70 mph

   B) 40 mph

   C) 60 mph

   D) 50 mph

4. **Q:** In a pie chart showing monthly expenses, if the rent slice covers 90°, what percentage of the monthly costs is the rent?

   A) 10%

   B) 15%

   C) 25%

   D) 30%

5. **Q:** If a bar graph shows that Company A made $400,000 in 2019 and $480,000 in 2020, by what percentage did their earnings increase?

   A) 15%

   B) 20%

   C) 25%

   D) 10%

6. **Q:** A ratio of blue to red balls in a bag is 3:4. If there are 12 blue balls, how many red balls are there?

   A) 16

   B) 8

   C) 18

   D) 9

7. **Q:** A table shows a 10% growth in a population every year. If a city has 50,000 people now, how many will it have after 1 year?

   A) 52,500

   B) 55,000

   C) 60,000

   D) 65,000

8. **Q:** If a company made a profit of $10 million in January and $15 million in February, by what percentage did the profit increase from January to February?

   A) 40%

   B) 50%

   C) 60%

   D) 70%

9. **Q:** A scatter plot shows a positive correlation between hours studied and exam scores. What can be inferred?

   A) Studying longer results in lower scores.

   B) There is no relation between studying and scores.

   C) Studying longer results in higher scores.

   D) The exam was too easy.

10. **Q:** Which operation is the inverse of multiplication?

    A) Addition

    B) Division

    C) Subtraction

    D) Exponentiation

11. **Q:** If a store sells a laptop for $1,200, marking a 20% profit, what was the price for the store?

    A) $1,000

    B) $960

    C) $1,100

    D) $1,020

12. Q: In a bar chart where the value for 2019 is half of the deal for 2020, if 2020's weight is 80, what is 2019's value?

A) 60

B) 50

C) 40

D) 20

13. Q: A store offers 15% off on all items during a sale. If a jacket costs $100, how much will it cost during the sale?

A) $75

B) $85

C) $90

D) $95

14. Q: If 30% of a number is 60, what is 20% of that number?

A) 30

B) 40

C) 50

D) 20

15. Q: A table of values shows that the total profit increases as the number of products sold increases. What type of correlation is this?

A) Positive correlation

B) Negative correlation

C) No correlation

D) Zero correlation

16. Q: The ratio of cats to dogs in a survey of pet owners is 4:5. If there are 80 cats, how many dogs are there?

A) 90

B) 100

C) 110

D) 70

17. Q: In a linear graph, if the line rises from left to right, it shows:

A) A negative slope

B) A positive slope

C) Zero slope

D) An undefined slope

18. Q: If a product's price increases by 25% and decreases by 25%, does it return to its original price?

   A) Yes

   B) No

   C) It becomes half

   D) It doubles

19. Q: If the average of five numbers is 25, what's their sum?

   A) 100

   B) 125

   C) 150

   D) 175

20. Q: A pie chart divides a company's expenses into various sections. If the team for "Utilities" takes up a third of the chart, how many degrees does this section represent?

   A) 90

   B) 120

   C) 60

   D) 180

21. Q: A company's profit grows by 15% each year. If the gain is $10,000 this year, approximately how much will it be the next year?

   A) $10,500

   B) $11,000

   C) $11,500

   D) $12,000

22. Q: A line graph shows a steady decrease in sales from January to June. What could be a possible reason for this trend?

   A) Increased advertising

   B) Product recalls

   C) Decreased product prices

   D) Increase in stock

23. Q: If a scatter plot displays no discernible pattern or trend between two variables, it can be concluded that:

   A) There's a strong positive correlation.

   B) There's a strong negative correlation.

   C) There's a weak correlation.

   D) The variables are independent of each other.

24. Q: In a graph showing a company's monthly sales, if the point for May is above the point for April, this means:

A) Sales decreased in May.

B) Sales remained the same in May.

C) Sales increased in May.

D) Sales data for May is inaccurate.

25. Q: What is the percentage decrease if a product's price decreased from $40 to $30?

A) 20%

B) 25%

C) 30%

D) 15%

ANSWER KEY

No more second-guessing! Our Answer Key section provides definitive answers to the questions presented in the Practice Test section. Each solution is not just about stating the correct option but also offering a brief explanation, ensuring you know the 'what' and the 'why' behind each response. This is a valuable tool for self-assessment, allowing readers to identify areas of strength and those that might need further study.

GENERAL KNOWLEDGE

1. **Correct Answer: C)** The U.S. Constitution

   Reason: The U.S. Constitution lays out the framework for the United States federal government, including its three branches and their respective powers.

2. **Correct Answer: C)** Grover Cleveland

   Reason: Grover Cleveland is the only President to serve two non-consecutive terms (22nd and 24th president).

3. **Correct Answer: A)** Judicial Review

   Reason: Judicial Review, established in Marbury v. Madison, allows the judiciary to examine and invalidate government actions that don't comply with the Constitution.

4. **Correct Answer: C)** Thomas Jefferson

   Reason: Thomas Jefferson was the principal author of the Declaration of Independence.

5. **Correct Answer: A)** 100

   Reason: The U.S. Senate has two members from each of the 50 states, making 100 senators.

6. **Correct Answer: C)** Abraham Lincoln

   Reason: Abraham Lincoln served as President from 1861 to 1865, encompassing the Civil War's duration.

7. **Correct Answer: A)** 1917

   Reason: The U.S. declared war on Germany and entered World War I in 1917.

8. **Correct Answer: A)** 19th amendment

   Reason: The 19th Amendment to the U.S. Constitution granted women the right to vote, prohibiting voter discrimination based on gender.

9. **Correct Answer: B)** The House of Representatives

   Reason: The House of Representatives has the sole power to impeach, while the Senate holds the trial and can convict the impeached official.

10. **Correct Answer: C)** Alexander Hamilton

    Reason: Alexander Hamilton was the first Secretary of the Treasury and laid the groundwork for the U.S. financial system.

11. **Correct Answer: D)** The Louisiana Purchase

    Reason: The Louisiana Purchase in 1803 nearly doubled the size of the U.S. by acquiring land from France.

12. **Correct Answer: B)** CIA

   Reason: The Central Intelligence Agency (CI**A)** is focused on foreign intelligence and counterintelligence operations.

13. **Correct Answer: C)** The sinking of the Maine

   Reason: The sinking of the USS Maine in Havana Harbor was a significant factor, leading the U.S. to declare war on Spain.

14. **Correct Answer: A)** John F. Kennedy

   Reason: John F. Kennedy was President during the Cuban Missile Crisis 1962.

15. **Correct Answer: C)** Alexander Hamilton

   Reason: While Madison, Jay, and Hamilton all wrote Federalist Papers, Hamilton wrote most of them.

16. **Correct Answer: B)** 1929

   Reason: The stock market crashed in October 1929, marking the beginning of the Great Depression.

17. **Correct Answer: C)** Plessy v. Ferguson

   Reason: The "separate but equal" doctrine was established in Plessy v. Ferguson in 1896, although it was later overturned by Brown v. Board of Education in 1954.

18. **Correct Answer: A)** 13th amendment

   Reason: The 13th Amendment, ratified in 1865, abolished slavery throughout the United States.

19. **Correct Answer: B)** Enforcing laws

   Reason: The Executive Branch, headed by the President, enforces and implements laws.

20. **Correct Answer: D)** Battles of Lexington and Concord

   Reason: The Battles of Lexington and Concord in April 1775 marked the start of the Revolutionary War.

21. **Correct Answer: A)** Hawaii

   Reason: Hawaii became the 50th state to join the Union on August 21, 1959.

22. **Correct Answer: B)** The House of Representatives

   Reason: The House of Representatives holds the "power of the purse," meaning they initiate revenue and appropriations bills.

23. **Correct Answer: B)** Unreasonable searches and seizures

   Reason: The 4th Amendment protects against unwarranted searches and seizures without probable cause.

24. **Correct Answer: A)** Impressment of American sailors

   Reason: One of the significant causes of the War of 1812 was the British impressment of American sailors into their navy.

25. **Correct Answer: B)** The Paris Agreement

   Reason: The Paris Agreement, adopted in 2015, seeks to address climate change by limiting global warming.

26. **Correct Answer: C)** Speaker of the House

   Reason: The line of succession is Vice President, Speaker of the House, President pro tempore of the Senate, and then various Cabinet positions, starting with the Secretary of State.

27. Correct Answer: C) Marbury v. Madison

Reason: Marbury v. Madison (1803) established that the judiciary can declare laws unconstitutional.

28. Correct Answer: B) 435

Reason: There are 435 voting members in the U.S. House of Representatives.

29. Correct Answer: C) Racial equality and the end of Jim Crow segregation

Reason: The main focus of the Civil Rights Movement in the 1960s was to achieve racial equality and end the system of Jim Crow segregation in the South.

30. Correct Answer: B) Lyndon B. Johnson

Reason: Lyndon B. Johnson signed the Civil Rights Act of 1964 to end segregation in public places and banned employment discrimination.

31. Correct Answer: C) Abraham Lincoln

Reason: Abraham Lincoln signed the Emancipation Proclamation in 1863, which declared that all enslaved people in Confederate-held territory were to be set free. This was a pivotal move during the Civil War and a significant step towards ending slavery in the U.S.

32. Correct Answer: C) Interpret laws

Reason: The Judicial Branch, primarily represented by the Supreme Court, is responsible for interpreting laws and ensuring they are consistent with the U.S. Constitution. This branch does not create or enforce laws but ensures that they are applied justly.

33. Correct Answer: C) Thomas Jefferson

Reason: While several Founding Fathers contributed to the Declaration of Independence, Thomas Jefferson is credited as the principal author. This document was drafted in 1776 and announced the American colonies' intent to separate from British rule.

34. Correct Answer: A) First

Reason: The First Amendment to the U.S. Constitution guarantees several fundamental rights, including freedom of speech, religion, press, assembly, and petition. These protections are foundational to American democracy and individual liberties.

35. Correct Answer: A) 1920s

Reason: U.S. women achieved the right to vote with the ratification of the 19th Amendment in 1920. This culminated in a long-fought suffrage movement that sought equal voting rights for women.

36. Correct Answer: D) James Madison

Reason: James Madison earned the title "Father of the Constitution" because of his pivotal role in drafting and promoting the U.S. Constitution and the Bill of Rights. He was also a key figure during the Constitutional Convention of 1787.

37. Correct Answer: C) It conducts the impeachment trial.

Reason: In the U.S. impeachment process, the House of Representatives can impeach or bring charges against the President. If this occurs, the U.S. Senate then conducts an impeachment trial to determine whether the President should be removed from office.

38. Correct Answer: B) The Montgomery Bus Boycott

Reason: The Montgomery Bus Boycott, initiated after Rosa Parks' refusal to give up her seat, is widely considered the event that sparked the modern Civil Rights Movement. The boycott lasted for over a year and highlighted systemic racial segregation and discrimination in the U.S.

39. Correct Answer: B) Three

Reason: The U.S. government operates with a system of checks and balances spread across three branches: Executive (President and Cabinet), Legislative (Congress: Senate and House of Representatives), and Judicial (Supreme Court and other federal courts).

40. Correct Answer: D) The Senate

Reason: While the President is the Commander-in-Chief of the armed forces, only Congress, specifically the Senate, can declare war. This division ensures a system of checks and balances in decision-making during potential conflict situations.

41. Correct Answer: B) Alexander Hamilton, James Madison, and John Jay

Reason: The Federalist Papers, a series of 85 essays advocating for the ratification of the U.S. Constitution, were written under the pseudonym "Publius" by Alexander Hamilton, James Madison, and John Jay.

42. Correct Answer: C) South Carolina

Reason: South Carolina was the first state to secede from the Union in December 1860, setting the stage for several other Southern states to follow suit and ultimately leading to the American Civil War.

43. Correct Answer: C) Enforce laws

Reason: The primary role of the Executive branch, which includes the President, Vice President, and Cabinet, is to enforce and uphold the laws passed by the Legislative Branch.

44. Correct Answer: B) The first ten amendments to the U.S. Constitution

Reason: The Bill of Rights comprises the first ten amendments to the U.S. Constitution, ensuring fundamental rights and protections for American citizens. These rights range from freedom of speech to protections against unreasonable searches and seizures.

45. Correct Answer: B) Franklin D. Roosevelt

Reason: Franklin D. Roosevelt introduced the New Deal, a series of programs, public work projects, and financial reforms, in response to the economic downturn of the Great Depression. The New Deal aimed to provide relief and recovery from the economic crisis.

46. Correct Answer: D) Marbury v. Madison

Reason: The 1803 Supreme Court case Marbury v. Madison established the principle of judicial review, granting the judiciary the power to strike down unconstitutional laws.

47. Correct Answer: B) The Vice President of the United States

Reason: The United States Vice President holds the title of President of the Senate. In this capacity, they can cast a tie-breaking vote but do not regularly participate in Senate debates.

48. Correct Answer: A) 13th amendment

Reason: The 13th Amendment to the U.S. Constitution, ratified in 1865, abolished slavery in all states and territories, marking a profound change in American society and rights.

49. Correct Answer: C) 9

Reason: The U.S. Supreme Court consists of nine justices: one Chief Justice and eight Associate Justices. This composition has remained consistent since the late 19th century, though the number was only sometimes set at nine.

50. Correct Answer: C) Updating Congress on national issues and setting an agenda

Reason: The State of the Union address, delivered annually by the President, updates Congress on the state of national affairs and sets forth the administration's legislative agenda and priorities. It provides an overview of the country's progress and challenges and the President's vision for the upcoming year.

OFFICE SKILLS

1. **Correct Answer**: **C)** M.S. PowerPoint

   Reason: M.S. PowerPoint is designed for creating slideshows and presentations.

2. **Correct Answer: C)** SMTP

   Reason: SMTP stands for Simple Mail Transfer Protocol, used to send emails.

3. **Correct Answer: B)** Calendar

   Reason: A calendar tool, especially in office suites, helps determine participants' availability.

4. **Correct Answer: C)** .zip

   Reason: The .zip extension usually represents compressed files or folders.

5. **Correct Answer: C)** Database

   Reason: Databases are designed for structured data storage, including contact information.

6. **Correct Answer: C)** Listen actively and empathetically

   Reason: Active and empathetic listening helps understand the client's concerns and fosters a constructive dialogue.

7. **Correct Answer: A)** CRM

   Reason: CRM is Customer Relationship Management, used for managing customer interactions.

8. **Correct Answer: B)** To hide recipients from each other

   Reason: BCC (Blind Carbon Copy) is used to send emails without displaying all the recipients.

9. **Correct Answer: C)** Virtual Private Network

   Reason: A VPN, or Virtual Private Network, creates a secure connection to another network over the internet.

10. **Correct Answer: C)** .xls

    Reason: .xls is an extension for Excel spreadsheet files, not images.

11. **Correct Answer: C)** The time difference

    Reason: The time difference ensures the call is scheduled conveniently for all parties.

12. **Correct Answer: C)** Identifying yourself and the organization

    Reason: Identifying oneself and the organization when answering a call is professional and courteous.

13. **Correct Answer: B)** Blocking unauthorized access

    Reason: A firewall is designed to block unauthorized access while permitting outward communication.

14. **Correct Answer: D)** Take time to understand their question or concern thoroughly

    Reason: Understanding a customer's problem fully before offering solutions is essential.

15. **Correct Answer: C)** Adobe Photoshop

    Reason: Adobe Photoshop is a graphic design and image editing software and is not part of the M.S. Office Suite.

16. **Correct Answer: C)** Software used to navigate the internet

    Reason: A browser is software for accessing and navigating the World Wide Web.

17. **Correct Answer: A)** A folder within another folder

    Reason: A sub-folder is contained within a primary or parent folder in hierarchical systems.

18. **Correct Answer: C)** Remain calm and try to address their concerns

    Reason: Maintaining professionalism, remaining calm, and trying to assist the customer is essential.

19. **Correct Answer: B)** Trello

    Reason: Trello is a popular project management tool used to organize tasks and teams.

20. **Correct Answer: B)** Stable internet connection

    Reason: A stable internet connection ensures seamless communication during video conferences.

21. **Correct Answer: C)** Google Docs

    Reason: Google Docs allows multiple users to collaborate on a document in real-time.

22. **Correct Answer: C)** Detecting and removing malicious software

    Reason: Antivirus software is designed to detect, prevent, and remove malicious software.

23. **Correct Answer: B)** To maintain professionalism and show respect to the sender

    Reason: Prompt responses indicate that you value communication and respect the sender's time.

24. **Correct Answer: C)** Storing data on remote servers accessed via the internet

    Reason: Cloud storage refers to storing data on remote servers which can be accessed online.

25. **Correct Answer: D)** Carbon Copy

    Reason: In email context, "CC" stands for Carbon Copy, used to send a copy of the message to additional recipients.

26. **Correct Answer: B)** To ensure clarity and show that you've understood their issue

    Reason: Repeating or paraphrasing confirms understanding and ensures both parties are on the same page.

27. **Correct Answer: B)** M.S. Excel

    Reason: M.S. Excel is designed to handle, analyze, and present numerical data.

28. **Correct Answer: D)** Frequently Asked Questions

    Reason: "FAQ" stands for Frequently Asked Questions, a typical section in websites or guides addressing common inquiries.

29. **Correct Answer: C)** To organize and categorize files for easy access

    Reason: Folders and subfolders help keep digital workspaces organized and make file retrieval more efficient.

30. **Correct Answer: C)** To protect against data loss due to unforeseen events or technical issues

    Reason: Regular backups ensure data safety during hardware failures, cyberattacks, or other unforeseen problems.

VERBAL SKILLS

1. **Correct Answer**: **B)** Malevolent

   Reason: "Malevolent" means having or showing a wish to harm others, which is the opposite of "benevolent".

2. **Correct Answer: B)** Adverb

   Reason: "Furiously" describes how the tail wagged, making it an adverb.

3. **Correct Answer: C)** Believe

   Reason: "Believe" follows the "i before e, except after c" rule.

4. **Correct Answer: C)** Introduce the topic and provide background

   Reason: The introduction provides context and previews the case for the reader.

5. **Correct Answer: C)** Future perfect

   Reason: The future perfect tense describes an action that will have been completed at some point in the future.

6. **Correct Answer: D)** They're going to the beach.

   Reason: "They're" is the contraction for "they are."

7. **Correct Answer: C)** Detailed support for the thesis statement

   Reason: The body of an essay provides evidence and arguments to support the thesis.

8. **Correct Answer: C)** Simple

   Reason: "Arduous" means requiring much effort and hard work.

9. **Correct Answer: C)** It's a sunny day, isn't it?

   Reason: "It's" is a contraction for "it is", and questions should end with a question mark.

10. **Correct Answer: B)** Summarize and reinforce the main points

    Reason: A conclusion recaps and emphasizes the essay's main ideas.

11. **Correct Answer: A)** Quickly

    Reason: "Quickly" describes how an action is performed.

12. **Correct Answer: C)** Common and of little value

    Reason: This idiom means something is standard and not unique.

13. **Correct Answer: A)** Adjective

    Reason: Adjectives describe nouns, while pronouns replace them.

14. **Correct Answer: C)** Discuss both similarities and differences

    Reason: "Compare and contrast" means discussing how items are alike and different.

15. **Correct Answer: C)** Possessive pronoun

    Reason: "Its" indicates possession, similar to "his" or "her".

16. **Correct Answer: A)** The cake is delicious; it's chocolate.

    Reason: Semicolons can connect closely related independent clauses.

17. **Correct Answer: B)** Clearly state the main idea or argument

    Reason: A thesis sets the direction for the essay by saying the main point.

18. **Correct Answer: B)** Scream

    Reason: The relationship is about the volume or clarity of speaking.

19. **Correct Answer: B)** Is walking

    Reason: A verb phrase includes the main verb and its auxiliaries.

20. **Correct Answer: B)** They're going over there to get their backpacks.

    Reason: "They're" is a contraction for "they are," "there" indicates a place, and "their" is a possessive pronoun.

21. **Correct Answer: C)** Malevolent

    Reason: "Benevolent" describes someone kind and well-meaning. Its antonym, "malevolent," refers to someone who has or shows a wish to do evil to others. The nature of antonyms is to provide contrasting meanings, making 'malevolent' the correct opposite.

22. **Correct Answer: B)** I love their new song.

    Reason: 'Their' is a possessive pronoun that denotes ownership or belonging. In the provided options, the sentence "I love their new song" correctly uses 'their' to indicate possession, suggesting the song belongs to them.

23. **Correct Answer: D)** To present the main idea

    Reason: A thesis statement succinctly presents an essay's primary point or argument. It provides a roadmap for the reader about what the article will discuss and argue, setting the tone and direction for the entire piece.

24. **Correct Answer: D)** The cats chased their tails.

    Reason: This sentence is structurally sound. It correctly employs the plural noun "cats" with the action they're undertaking, and it uses the possessive "their" appropriately to indicate that the tails belong to the cats.

25. **Correct Answer: C)** Supporting details and evidence

    Reason: The body of an essay delves deeper into the arguments or points made in the introduction. It's where you provide supporting facts, Reasons, and evidence to support the main idea or thesis statement.

26. **Correct Answer: B)** She wanted to complement his work.

    Reason: The sentence likely intended to use "compliment," meaning to praise, rather than "complement," which means something that completes or goes well with something.

27. **Correct Answer: C)** Drawing a conclusion based on given information

    Reason: Inference in reading comprehension refers to the ability to deduce or conclude something that isn't explicitly stated in the text but is implied by the given information. It's a crucial skill that allows readers to grasp the more profound meaning or subtext.

28. **Correct Answer: C)** "How are you feeling?" he inquired.

    Reason: The sentence correctly places the question mark inside the quotation marks and follows standard grammar rules for punctuating direct speech in written content.

29. **Correct Answer: C)** Summarize the main points and restate the thesis in a new way

    Reason: The conclusion of an essay serves as a wrap-up, providing a concise summary of the arguments presented and restating the thesis to reinforce the main idea, but often in a manner that feels conclusive or slightly different than how it was initially introduced.

30. **Correct Answer: D)** The movie was too long for my liking.

    Reason: The word 'too' can be used as an adverb to mean "in addition" or "more than is desirable." In the given sentence, 'too' is correctly used to indicate an excess, suggesting the movie's length was more than what the speaker found desirable.

31. Correct Answer: D) An argumentative text

Reason: An argumentative text or essay is structured to present an argument and persuade the reader to accept a particular point of view. It typically involves presenting evidence, facts, and logical reasoning to support the writer's stance.

32. Correct Answer: C) Accommodate

Reason: "Accommodate" is the only word spelled correctly among the provided options. Spelling is a fundamental aspect of writing, and knowing the correct spellings of common words is essential for clear and effective communication.

33. Correct Answer: A) The dog wagged its tail.

Reason: 'Its' is a possessive pronoun used to denote ownership or belonging. In the sentence "The dog wagged its tail," 'its' correctly indicates that the tail belongs to the dog.

34. Correct Answer: C) Understand the meaning of an unfamiliar word or phrase

Reason: Context clues are bits of information or words surrounding a foreign word or phrase that can help readers discern its meaning. These clues can be examples, synonyms, antonyms, or the general sense of the surrounding text.

35. Correct Answer: B) The chef cooked the meal.

Reason: In passive voice, the object of the action becomes the sentence's subject. The sentence "The chef cooked the meal" is inactive because the meal (the thing of the action) is now the focus or subject of the sentence, while the doer of the action (the chef) becomes secondary.

36. Correct Answer: C) The overall point or message the author is conveying

Reason: A text's 'main idea' captures its essence, summarizing what the text is primarily about. It represents the overarching theme or message that the author wishes to communicate to readers.

37. Correct Answer: B) To whom should I address the letter?

Reason: 'Whom' is an object pronoun, which refers to the person an action is being done to. In the sentence "To whom should I address the letter?", 'whom' is correctly used as the object of the preposition 'to'.

38. Correct Answer: C) Introducing the main topic and capturing the reader's interest

Reason: The introduction of an essay sets the stage for what's to come. Its primary purpose is to introduce the topic while grabbing the reader's attention, often with a hook or engaging statement. This helps set the tone and provides context for the rest of the essay.

39. Correct Answer: C) Beautiful

Reason: An adjective is a word that describes or modifies a noun. In the provided sentence, "beautiful" describes the noun "dress," indicating its appearance or quality, and thus is an adjective.

40. Correct Answer: C) Flows logically and is easy to follow

Reason: Coherence in writing ensures that ideas are organized and connected in a way that provides a clear, logical progression for the reader. This helps in understanding the content and the relationships between the presented ideas.

MATHEMATICAL ABILITIES

1. **Correct Answer: A)** 30

   Reason: 12% of 250 = 0.12 x 250 = 30.

2. **Correct Answer: B)** $40

   Reason: 20% of $50 = $10. Thus, $50 - $10 = $40.

3. **Correct Answer: C)** 60 mph

   Reason: Speed = Distance/Time. So, 360 miles/6 hours = 60 mph.

4. **Correct Answer: C)** 25%

   Reason: A full circle is 360°. 90° is a quarter of that, representing 25% of the whole.

5. **Correct Answer: B)** 20%

   Reason: Increase = $480,000 - $400,000 = $80,000. Percentage increase = ($80,000/$400,000) x 100 = 20%.

6. **Correct Answer: A)** 16

   Reason: If 3 parts represent 12 balls, then 1 part represents 4 balls. Hence, 4 parts (for red balls) represent 16 balls.

7. **Correct Answer: B)** 55,000

   Reason: 10% of 50,000 is 5,000. Adding that to the original number gives 55,000.

8. **Correct Answer: B)** 50%

   Reason: The increase is $5 million, which is 50% of January's $10 million.

9. **Correct Answer: C)** Studying longer results in higher scores.

   Reason: A positive correlation indicates that as one variable increases, the other also increases.

10. **Correct Answer: B)** Division

    Reason: Division undoes multiplication in the same way subtraction undoes addition.

11. **Correct Answer: A)** $1,000

    Reason: If $1,200 represents 120% (100% original cost + 20% profit), 1% is $1,200/120 = $10. So, 100% (actual cost) is $10 x 100 = $1,000.

12. **Correct Answer: C)** 40

    Reason: Half of 80 is 40. Hence, if 2020's value is represented by 80, then 2019's is represented by 40.

13. **Correct Answer: B)** $85

    Reason: A 15% discount on $100 is $15. Subtracting this discount from the original price: $100 - $15 = $85.

14. **Correct Answer: B)** 40

    Reason: If 30% represents 60, then 1% is 60/30 = 2. Thus, 20% is 20 x 2 = 40.

15. **Correct Answer: A)** Positive correlation

    Reason: If both variables (products sold and profit) increase together, it's a positive correlation.

16. **Correct Answer: B)** 100

    Reason: If 4 parts represent 80 cats, then 1 represents 20. Hence, 5 parts (for dogs) represent 100.

17. Correct Answer: B) A positive slope

Reason: A line that rises from left to right on a graph has a positive slope, meaning as one variable increases, the other also does.

18. Correct Answer: B) No

Reason: After a 25% increase, the price becomes 125% of the original. A 25% decrease on this new price does not return it to the original. Instead, it becomes 75% of the increased cost.

19. Correct Answer: B) 125

Reason: The average of numbers is the sum divided by the count of numbers. If the average of five numbers is 25, their sum is 5 x 25 = 125.

20. Correct Answer: B) 120

Reason: A full circle in a pie chart represents 360 degrees. If the "Utilities" section is a third of the chart, it means 360/3 = 120 degrees.

21. Correct Answer: C) $11,500

Reason: A 15% growth on $10,000 results in an increase of $1,500. Adding this to the original profit, we get $10,000 + $1,500 = $11,500.

22. Correct Answer: B) Product recalls

Reason: Product recalls often lead to a decline in trust among consumers, which can result in a drop in sales. While other options might impact sales, recalls usually have a more direct harmful effect.

23. Correct Answer: D) The variables are independent of each other.

Reason: A scatter plot with no discernible trend suggests that changes in one variable do not predict changes in the other, implying that they are independent.

24. Correct Answer: C) Sales increased in May.

Reason: In most graphs representing time-based data, a higher point for one month compared to the previous one indicates an increase in the represented quantity for that month.

25. Correct Answer: B) 25%

Reason: The decrease is $10, and $10 is 25% of the original price of $40. Thus, the product's price decreased by 25%.

FREQUENTLY ASKED QUESTIONS

Q: What is the primary focus of "Explorations in Verbal and Mathematical Skills"?

A: The book delves deep into honing verbal skills—like reading comprehension, grammar, and essay writing—and mathematical abilities, such as arithmetic, data interpretation, and real-world problem-solving.

Q: Who is the target audience for this book?

A: Anyone from students seeking academic excellence, professionals aiming to brush up their skills, to educators looking for comprehensive material can benefit from this book.

Q: How is the book structured?

A: The book is divided into sections based on different skill sets, each containing theory, examples, and practice exercises to solidify understanding.

Q: Are there any practice exercises or sample problems included?

A: Yes, after each chapter, readers will find practice questions tailored to test and reinforce the concepts discussed.

Q: Can this book help with standardized testing preparation?

A: Absolutely! The book is designed to align with many of the concepts tested in standardized exams, making it a valuable resource for preparation.

Q: Is prior knowledge required before reading this book?

A: While having a basic understanding might help, the book is written approachable, ensuring beginners can also grasp the concepts.

Q: Are there any digital or online resources accompanying the book?

A: Yes, the book comes with an access code for online modules which include interactive exercises, video lessons, and additional resources.

Q: How often is the book updated with new content or methodologies?

A: The book goes through revisions approximately every two years, ensuring it stays updated with the latest educational methodologies and research.

Q: Who are the authors of "Explorations in Verbal and Mathematical Skills"?

A: The book is a collaborative effort of educators and researchers with decades of experience in language arts and mathematics.

Q: Can educators use this book as a classroom resource?

A: Certainly! Many educators have integrated this book into their curriculum due to its comprehensive approach.

Q: Are there solutions provided for the practice exercises?

A: Yes, at the end of the book, there's a solutions section detailing answers and methodologies for each exercise.

Q: Is this book suitable for self-study?

A: Absolutely. The book is structured to encourage self-paced learning, with clear explanations and step-by-step methodologies.

Q: How does the book approach the topic of essay writing?

A: Essay writing is covered extensively, from understanding prompts to structuring and crafting coherent, focused essays.

Q: Does the book only cater to American English rules and usage?

A: While the primary focus is on Standard American English, it also touches upon the differences and similarities with other English usages globally.

Q: Can I get this book in an e-book format?

A: "Explorations in Verbal and Mathematical Skills" is available in print and digital formats.

Q: How can I access the supplementary online modules?

A: Each copy of the book comes with a unique access code which can be used to register on the companion website and access the online resources.

Q: Is the book suitable for group study or workshops?

A: Yes, its format is adaptable for both individual and group settings, making it suitable for workshops, study groups, and classroom discussions.

Q: Are there any discounts for bulk purchases?

A: Educational institutions and workshops organizers can contact the publishers for information on bulk discounts.

Q: Does the book provide real-world applications of the concepts discussed?

A: Indeed, one of the book's strengths is its emphasis on applying verbal and mathematical concepts to real-world scenarios, ensuring practical understanding.

Q: How can I provide feedback or suggestions for the book?

A: Feedback is always welcome! There's a dedicated section on the book's companion website where readers can share their experiences and suggestions for future editions.

CONCLUSION

As we turn the final pages of this extensive guide, it's essential to take a moment to reflect on the journey we've undertaken together. From the intricacies of U.S. history to the nuances of verbal skills, from mastering mathematical concepts to understanding office protocols, this book has been a comprehensive tour of varied subjects essential for personal and professional development.

In an era marked by information overload, finding a consolidated, reliable, and well-researched source can be a daunting task. This book aimed to fill that gap, serving not just as a repository of knowledge, but also as a mentor guiding you through complex concepts, a trainer offering practice tests, and a confidant providing clear answers. It was designed to be both a starting point for beginners and a refresher for those who needed to revisit topics they might have once known.

The importance of continuous learning cannot be overstated in our fast-evolving world. It's not just about passing exams or acing interviews but about nurturing an inquisitive mind, fostering critical thinking, and being prepared for the unpredictable twists and turns of the future. While this book provides tools and resources, the true journey of learning is deeply personal and never-ending.

In conclusion, while this guide offers a foundation, the onus of building upon it lies with you, the reader. Embrace curiosity, never stop questioning, practice regularly, and always seek to expand the horizons of your knowledge. Remember, every great endeavor begins with a single step, and with this book in your arsenal, you're well-equipped to take many more. We hope you found value in these pages and wish you the very best in all your future academic and professional pursuits.

SPECIAL BONUS

D ear reader, I would be grateful if you would take a minute of your time and post a review on AMAZON to let other users know how this experience was and what you liked most about the book. Also, I have recently decided to give a *gift* to all our readers. Yes, I want to provide you with the assistance that will help you with your study you will receive

- **AUDIOBOOK (mp3 audio files)** from listening to whenever and wherever you want! Receive the accompanying **audiobook absolutely free!** Whether you're on the move, juggling tasks, or just seeking a varied study rhythm, this guide adapts to your unique needs.
- Unlock unparalleled insights into *U.S. governance, current events, office dynamics*, and more with our curated **set of 100 flashcards.** Crafted for the modern civil service aspirant, our set is available in a sleek**, print-ready PDF** as well as an interactive digital suite for the **ANKI app.** Dive into essential topics like the *influential roles of U.S. presidents, landmark Supreme Court rulings, and indispensable office protocols.* Elevate your civil service exam prep to new heights - a distinctive advantage, exclusive to our guide!

You can track your progress and conveniently and interactively memorize the most important terms and concepts! Download to your device: **Anki APP or AnkiDroid**, or enter the web page and register free of charge. Then import the files we have given you as a gift and use the flashcards whenever and wherever you want to study and track your progress.

Below you will find a **QR CODE** that will give you direct access to this bonus (file to download directly to your device) without having to subscribe to any mailing list or leave your personal information.

I hope you will appreciate it.

To communicate with us directly, please write to us at

booklovers.1001@gmail.com

We are waiting for your feedback on amazon, in any case!

A cordial greeting; we wish you all the best.

Thank you!

THANK YOU!

Made in United States
Orlando, FL
17 November 2023

39117652R00059